Separate Ways

Separate Ways

The Heart of Europe

Peter Shore

Duckworth

To my children and grandchildren.

First published in 2000 by
Gerald Duckworth & Co. Ltd
61 Frith Street, London W1D 3JL
Tel: 020 7434 4242
Fax: 020 7434 4420
Email: enquiries@duckworth-publishers.co.uk
www.ducknet.co.uk

A catalogue record for this book is available
from the British Library.

ISBN 0 7156 2972 7

Typeset by Derek Doyle & Associates, Liverpool.
Printed in Great Britain by
Biddles Ltd, www.biddles.co.uk

Contents

Calendar of Key Events

May 1945   World War II ends in Europe with the surrender of the German Armed Forces.

July - August 1945   Potsdam Conference attended by the US, USSR and UK, excluding France.

August 1945   Japan surrenders following US atom bomb attacks.

March 1947   President Truman declares US support for democracy everywhere.

May 1950   Robert Schuman calls for the merger of the coal and steel industries of France, Germany and other European states.

October 1949   NATO is formed, with the US and Canada joining the free European nations.

June 1950   Communist North Korea attacks South Korea.

November 1951   NATO meeting at Lisbon calls for 51 divisions in Europe, including West Germany to France's dismay.

May 1952   France, West Germany, Italy, Belgium, Holland and Luxembourg (The Six) establish the first European supranational entity, the European Coal and Steel Community (ECSC).

March 1954   The supranational European Defence Community treaty of the Six - which France sponsored since February 1952 - fails to win ratification by French Parliament on fears of German rearmament.

May – September 1955   The Messina Conference on European economic integration by the Six - no British Minister attends.

May 1956   Egypt's leader Nasser seizes the Suez Canal

March 1957   The Six sign the Treaty of Rome establishing a Common Market (EEC).

May 1958   De Gaulle returns to power in France and vetoes

	Britain's proposals for a European Free Trade Area.
October 1958	The UK forms a limited European Free Trade Area (EFTA) with Norway, Sweden, Denmark, Switzerland, Austria and Eire (The Seven).
June 1960	The Macmillan Government announces its intention to open negotiations with the Six for UK membership.
May 1961	The Soviet Union recognizes East Germany as a Sovereign State and erects the Berlin Wall.
January 1963	De Gaulle vetoes UK application for membership of the Common Market and signs the Franco-German Treaty.
1966	De Gaulle boycots meetings of the European Communities, establishing the veto on matters of national importance (the Luxembourg Compromise).
March 1967	The Wilson Government announces launch of UK's second attempt to join the Common Market; vetoed by de Gaulle in November.
July 1970	The Heath Government announces third British application for membership. In December 1971, Heath signs the Treaty of Accession. UK membership begins on 1 January 1973.
1974-5	The Wilson Government undertakes 'renegotiation' of terms of UK entry.
June 1975	UK holds its first nation-wide referendum on the European Community; a large majority votes to stay in.
1979	The European Communities agree, under Roy Jenkins Presidency of the European Commission, to establish European Monetary System and a Exchange Rate Mechanism (ERM). Britain declines to join ERM.
June 1984	Margaret Thatcher concludes four year campaign to reduce UK contribution to EC funds by halving the sums involved.
December 1985	The Single European Act greatly extends the Common Market and greatly reduces the right of veto for member states.

October 1989   The European Community approves outline plan of the Committee of Central Bankers, chaired by President Jacques Delors, to establish a European Single Currency.

November 1989   The Berlin Wall is demolished - the end of Communism in East Germany and in the whole of Eastern Europe.

October 1990   Britain joins the Exchange Rate Mechanism (ERM). In December 1990 John Major becomes Prime Minister.

November 1991   The Maastricht Treaty is completed: a major extension of competence of the EC into domestic policy and into external policy as well, and commitment to the Single Currency. UK opts out of Single Currency, the Social Chapter, and the Schengen agreement.

June 1992   The Danish Referendum rejects the Maastricht Treaty and the UK ratification Bill is suspended.

September 1992   Pound Sterling is forced to leave the Exchange Rate Mechanism (White or Black Wednesday according to taste). The Maastricht Treaty Bill finally passes through Parliament in December 1992.

June 1997   The Blair Government signs the Amsterdam Treaty, opening the way for a European Foreign and Security policy with an autonomous defence capacity to back it up.

December 1998   Blair and Chirac sign the St Malo Joint Declaration, committing both countries to new defence arrangements within the European Union.

December 1999   The Helsinki European Council agrees creation of a 'rapid reaction force', 60,000 strong, to back European Union foreign security policy.

Preface

I state in my introduction the reasons that have impelled me to write this book: above all the need to cast a searching light on the nature and direction of the European Union and – just as important – to refute the distortions, deceptions and downright lies with which, in the past forty years, the political establishment has bewildered the British people about themselves and their relations with Europe.

Here, I want to say what the book is about and why I believe every adult in our land, who has some regard for our country and its future, should at least read what it contains. I guarantee that much that has been hidden will be revealed; and that the reader will feel better, much better, about the present and future prospects of our land.

The first half of the book takes us from 1945, the end of the war, to the present day. It explains why it is that Britain and its European neighbours have pursued different aims since the defeat of Germany in May 1945. It examines the now habitual assertions about how Britain missed (according to taste) buses, trains and boats, and failed to seize the leadership of Europe to its own advantage. Instead it states the truth of the matter: that Britain pursued, with its US ally, an extended near-global role to help ensure security and stability world-wide while our neighbour France pursued a narrower policy for containing Germany and enmeshing it within a separate political and economic bloc in Western Europe, the European Community.

We co-existed without too much difficulty and with considerable shared purposes until 1960 when – following the humiliating failure to seize the Suez Canal in 1956 and a period of slow and weakening economic growth – there was an extraordinary failure of nerve in the British government and establishment that led to a complete reversal of UK policy: to a retreat from our Commonwealth and global connections and a quest, evermore urgent, to become a late member of the European Community.

From 1960 until the late 1980s, the story is one of Britain's repeated applications; evermore damaging terms of entry; our virtual capitulation when we joined in 1973 and thereafter a decade and more of reluctant membership as the UK found itself embarrassed and isolated by the on-going drive of our Continental neighbours for closer union. Mrs Thatcher's ill-considered Single Market initiative in the mid-1980s led – to her own exasperation – only to further expansion of the powers of the European Community and to a vast extension of qualified majority voting.

The third phase that brings us to the present, was opened by the fall of the Berlin Wall in 1989, the reunification of Germany, the collapse of communism in Eastern Europe and the major effort of Mitterand in France and Delors in Brussels to draw the re-united German state still closer together, in every area of policy, with its neighbours and partners in Europe. The result was the Maastricht Treaty, with its commitment to Economic and Monetary Union and the single currency and to a common foreign, security and defence policy.

So much for the first part of the book. The second part of the book looks at the options before us. First, it considers the choices available within Europe, with the clear prospect now of agreement on a two-tiered or multi-tiered Europe – a prospect enormously enhanced by the need to accommodate no less than twelve East European/ Mediterranean applicant nations.

Second, whatever options are agreed for our future relationships with the European Union, there are the no less important, and certainly stronger connections that exist outside Europe with the fifty-four members of the Commonwealth, with the English-speaking world, with the United States and with the United Nations where we remain a major player, one of the five permanent veto-wielding members of its Security Council. To discount these connections either as embarrassing remnants of the empire or as nostalgic Second World War ties – that can now be dispensed with at will and without harm to the nation – would be to profoundly misjudge their nature and strength. These connections are in fact rather more alive than our relations with Europe. The book concludes in the spirit though not the words that Franklin D. Roosevelt addressed to his fellow Americans in the Great Depression of the early 1930s: we have nothing to fear in, half-in, or outside the European Union, but fear itself.

When I first put pen to paper, I expected that the events and arguments of the 'Europhiles' would, to some extent, put me on the defensive. In the event, I have found that the balance of fact and argument is such that I can only marvel at the wisdom of Britain's great post-war leaders, Churchill and Attlee in keeping us outside the European integration movement; and equally at the stubborn resistance and belief in themselves of the majority of the British people in spite of the endless discouragement and bad political leadership of recent decades.

This then is an account of why the British people, the great enemies of tyranny and the champions of democracy, the inhabitants of what has been in truth a 'Blessed Plot', have reason indeed for confidence and a sober pride in their country. Having been so badly led in this past quarter-century, they must now demand of their still hesitant leaders new policies and new directions that will enable us to prosper in our own self-governing, independent democracy and to contribute in the years ahead to the affairs of mankind as we have done so much and for so long in the past.

Acknowledgements

Many have assisted me in the course of writing this book. I am particularly grateful to my old friends, Professor Norman McKenzie and Will Camp, and to my son Chris Shore, who read the whole in manuscript form, and to my House of Lords colleagues John Gilbert, Alun Chalfont and Daphne Park, whose judgement and expertise helped me with a particularly difficult chapter.

I would like to add my thanks too to all those who over the years and in numerous debates, in public meetings and in both Houses of Parliament, forced me to think and rethink the great issues of our future direction and purpose as a nation and a state.

I am grateful too to the Library staff of both the Lords and Commons in responding to my many requests for information, and of course to Stephen Hill, Chairman of Duckworth.

Finally, a special word of thanks to my long-term assistant and secretary Mrs Sylvia Padwick, without whose devoted help the book would never have been finished: and to my wife Liz for not only enduring my near-total preoccupation for a seven-month stretch, but also for allowing me to fill every surface, every ledge, every table in our house with mounds of papers and files.

Introduction

This is the book about Britain and Europe that I have long wanted to write. I have postponed this task not just because of human weakness and distractions but because the story is one to which new chapters are being constantly added as the pace of integration quickens and the scope of the European enterprise advances ever further. No one wants to write a work that is clearly outdated before the printers can do their work. On occasions, therefore, I have had to anticipate as well as to record.

I wanted to write it for several reasons. One is the enormous importance of the issues involved – they tower like giants above the dwarf issues of contemporary politics. They include self-government, independence, democracy and our future status as a country or a province.

Another reason is that, while many books have been written about Britain and its relations with Europe, there has been a remarkable failure to address and explain what the argument is all about. Why has Britain in the past half century made major decisions different from those of most of our continental neighbours? What are the real issues that divide us and what now are the choices before us?

To clarify and explain is a particularly urgent need at this moment because the agenda for major decisions includes items of exceptional importance: enlargement of membership from the present fifteen to twenty-seven or more and changes in the voting-power in the Council of Ministers. It will also include the extension in substance of the existing economic, monetary and political union into a new defence union equipped with its own armed forces, ready not only to defend its own territories from attack but also to project European military and economic power to enforce elsewhere its own Common Foreign and Security Policy.

These are reasons enough but I have additionally, in an unusually long span of direct experience and involvement in the politics of Britain and Europe, some insights and information which it is now sensible to place in the public domain.

Like others of my generation, I have lived through the Second World War, the defeat of Germany in 1945, the re-emergence of Europe from ruin to prosperity, the formation of NATO and the long years of the Cold War, the collapse of the Soviet Union in 1991 and the victory of the West – a period of quite remarkable and dramatic change in the fortunes of nations and the balance of world power.

I became directly involved in the Britain and Europe question in 1961 when the then Prime Minister, Harold Macmillan, made his historic announcement that the UK – in total reversal of its policies pursued between 1945 and 1960 – was now applying to join the European Community (the Common Market) as a full member. The then leader of the Labour Party, Hugh Gaitskell, at once asked my colleague, David Ennals, the International Secretary and myself, as head of the Labour Party Research Department, to examine the issues and present a preliminary paper for consideration by himself and his parliamentary colleagues.

It was then, with a genuinely open mind but with the background knowledge of events that all thinking people of my age group possessed, that I read that basic document, the Rome Treaty – it was difficult then even to obtain a copy in the English language – and made my first preliminary analysis of its contents. Forty years have passed since then and only in a few, relatively short, periods of time, have I found myself not involved with Europe and Europe-related issues. No: I didn't write that famous Conference speech when Hugh

Gaitskell summoned up a 'thousand years of British history' and recalled the courage and sacrifice of those Commonwealth forces who stood by us throughout the Second World War and at Vimy Ridge and Gallipoli in the First. But I did write the policy statement Gaitskell was recommending in his Brighton oration. After that I had frequent discussions on Europe with his successor Harold Wilson, both before and after he first became Prime Minister in 1964.

In 1967 I joined the Wilson Cabinet and happily accepted de Gaulle's second veto on our application to join. After Labour's narrow victory in March 1974, as Secretary of State for Trade, I took part in the 'renegotiation' of the terms of entry to which Labour had pledged itself, attending many Council of Ministers' meetings in Brussels. When the 'renegotiation' was concluded in 1975 and the referendum on its terms was held, I was one of the seven dissenting Cabinet Ministers who campaigned for a 'No' vote. I remained a Cabinet Minister at Trade until 1976 and then as Secretary of the Environment in the Callaghan government until its fall in March 1979. In Opposition again, I was first made Shadow Foreign Secretary and then Shadow Chancellor. I was not happy with the 1983 manifesto (the longest suicide note in history) but could certainly live, without distress, with one of its central policies: withdrawal from the Common Market. My period in the Shadow Cabinet ended in 1987. In the ten years that followed, before the 1997 election of the New Labour government, I served as the senior Labour Member on the House of Commons Select Committee on Foreign Affairs – with its wide remit to study not only European matters but also the great range of issues that involved the UK and its parliament in Southern Africa, the Gulf, Latin America and the Commonwealth.

Those last ten years in the House on the Foreign Affairs Select Committee I look back on with particular satisfaction. They helped me not only to keep in close touch with developing European issues but also enabled me to place Britain and Europe in the context of problems, conflicts, opportunities and interests not just in one continent, Europe, but in all six.

Finally I have one additional reason for writing that has acted as a spur and a goad whenever my resolution began to falter. The knowledge that, on these, the greatest issues before our people and our country, deception has been practised by successive governments on a scale, and over a prolonged period of time, without precedent in our modern history.

I use the words 'deceive' and 'deception' with care – and with reluctance. Honourable and serious men and women have argued the contrary case to my own, in favour of European integration, with integrity and force. I have no complaint against them. But they have not been the dominant voices in this prolonged debate.

And while in the past few years, there are signs that the public, some of the media and a growing minority of politicians are more alert, less gullible and more critical of things European than has been the case in most of the past forty years, the evidence of past misdeeds and worse must be recorded – if only to reduce the dangers of their repetition in the period directly ahead.

Let me preface what follows with two admissions. First, as a convinced and long-term Eurosceptic,* I recognise that my judgement is bound to be tilted by my own convictions. Second, I am well aware of the danger when strong convictions are involved that those who hold them are tempted, when faced with adverse events, to allege 'conspiracy' – in short, to be paranoid. Because of this obvious danger, my account of the deception of the British people is drawn almost exclusively from now unquestioned facts and from recent statements made, not by my *allies* but by my *opponents* in the debate.

In this, I have been greatly assisted by the passage of time. The 30-year rule on the non-disclosure of Cabinet records is still in force but the documents relating to that very important decade, 1960-70, when the governments of Macmillan and Wilson made their separate

4

applications for UK entry to the Common Market, are now available.

No less important are the still growing flood of memoirs by those politicians and others most involved in European affairs, not only in the 1960s but in subsequent decades. Contemporary historians and investigatory journalists have been particularly helpful. In what follows, I shall draw heavily on a number of recent works, including Hugo Young's *This Blessed Plot* (1998) in the preparation of which the author had access to very interesting and still unpublished Foreign Office documents; Larkin and Oliver's *A Discreet Word: Britain's Secret Propaganda During the Cold War* (1998); and particularly most recently, in February 2000, that remarkable BBC radio programme based on interviews by Christopher Cook with now mainly retired politicians and senior officials, intimately involved in European events, as well as serious academic scholars and researchers.

This most recent material has given fresh evidence and authority to what previously had been considered as no more than interesting, if worrying, allegations and at the same time has brought to light some relevant matters not previously even guessed at. Further, this material has the great advantage and value that the authors and presenters are either European enthusiasts and federalists like Hugo Young or – to the best of my knowledge – professional and quite uncommitted researchers and interviewers.

What has been revealed is: first, improper behaviour by Foreign Office officials and civil servants; second the abuse by very senior BBC executives and producers of their Charter obligation to ensure neutrality and even-handiness in presenting politically controversial issues; and third the encouragement – and organisation – of this improper conduct by senior ministers and politicians.

I begin with the astonishing story of misbehaviour by a senior Foreign Office official, Mr John Robinson. An account appeared in 1980, as part of Douglas Jay's memoirs, *Change and Fortune* but a far fuller version is to be found in Hugo Young's *This Blessed Plot*. Mr Robinson was a European expert and enthusiast who had served in Brussels as part of Edward Heath's team in the 1961-3 negotiations – a man promoted to head the European Integration Department in the late 1960s. The French President, de Gaulle, had vetoed the UK's second application for entry to the European Community some fifteen months earlier when our Ambassador in Paris was granted the unusual privilege of a lunchtime meeting with the President. Our Ambassador Christopher Soames was not a career diplomat but a senior politician, a former Conservative Cabinet Minister, and of course son-in-law of Winston Churchill. He and de Gaulle lunched together on 4 February 1969 and the President talked – according to reports it was more a monologue than a dialogue – with the frankness that is normally reserved for interchanges between political leaders.

What de Gaulle put forward was a line of thought about Britain and Europe and the future that would have been music to the ears of any previous UK government including Macmillan's: a Europe rid of the supranational pretentions of the Treaties, a Europe based on sovereign states, a Europe '*de patries*'. And while there was no hint that the UK would be allowed to join – de Gaulle was determined to dominate the Six, with his junior partner West Germany – what was clearly suggested was an industrial free trade area, with no obligation on the UK to impose the common external tariff on Commonwealth and other suppliers or to import high-cost continental food.

Soames at once cabled London where it reached No 10 just as Harold Wilson was about to visit Bonn for a pre-arranged bilateral meeting with Chancellor Kiesinger there. The question at once arose, should the Prime Minister mention the Paris conversation in his own talks in Bonn? More seriously, was it a genuine initiative, or a ploy whose ultimate publication would embarrass the UK with its continued efforts to gain admission?

Wilson's instinct was to say nothing but he decided, shortly before departure, to make a passing reference to it and asked the Foreign Office for 'a few simple sentences' to be included in his briefing. Mr Robinson and his European Integration Department decided otherwise. He sent instead a full report of the de Gaulle/Soames conversation, together with a memo to be used in the meeting with the German Chancellor.

Wilson, in his memoirs, says he was 'furious' – and of course didn't use it. But that was only the beginning of Robinson's truly disgraceful conduct. He dispatched the report of the Paris talks not only to Wilson at the British Embassy in Bonn but simultaneously and *en clair* to all relevant British Embassies in Europe. As intended, the fact and nature of the conversation soon became public knowledge. Questions were directed to Paris from other member states and from journalists from everywhere.

The French responded with a very sketchy account of what had taken place in the newspaper, *Le Figaro*. Whereupon, according to Hugo Young's applauding account, the 'Foreign Office chief spokesman in London summoned selected correspondents to "correct" the French account. He read to them, verbatim, large chunks of Soames's original dispatch, giving rise to an international furore that put paid to anything serious that de Gaulle might have had in mind.'

It was clearly deliberate. I was in Cabinet at the time and I can remember – just – the matter being reported to colleagues by the then Foreign Secretary, a convert to the European cause, Michael Stewart. The item was brief, the account heavily slanted by suggestions of deliberate French trickery. No disciplinary action was taken. Clearly, Robinson enjoyed a close and protective relationship with top FCO officials. He was, as Hugo Young describes him, part of a 'militant vanguard', an 'elite regiment' of committed Europhiles, then taking key positions in the FCO. There are reasons to fear a number of them, including those they have recruited, are there still.

The next episode is one that, while its authenticity is both unquestionable and unquestioned, I find even now difficult to believe. I refer to the notorious 'media breakfasts', arranged at Prime Minister Heath's request in 1970 by the former Central Office Publicity Officer, Geoffrey Tucker, with the unambiguous task of trying to shift public opinion in the UK from opposition to support of entry to the Common Market.

The coming together, in regular weekly breakfast meetings, at the Connaught Hotel of ministers, leading opposition politicians, senior industrialists, the European Movement (EM) and friendly journalists is itself an unusual occurrence but not a sufficient cause for censure or concern. What distinguished and set the Connaught Breakfast apart were three things: first the presence there of senior Foreign Office officials in the persons of Norman Reddaway, Head of the Information Research Department (the IRD) – with its close links to the intelligence services – his assistant Tommy Tucker, head of the Editorial Section of the IRD, and Crispin Tickell, the top personal civil service aide to the negotiating minister, Geoffrey Rippon; second, the regular attendance of senior BBC executives, specifically the Managing Director of BBC Radio, Ian Trethowan, the Director/Producer of the Today Programme, Marshall Stewart and, from ITN News-at-Ten, Nigel Ryan.

From the government's point of view, these were most valuable contacts. The Today Programme, with its eight million listeners, then as now helped set the agenda for both the day's events and for subsequent BBC news and current affair programmes, while News-at-Ten, with its still larger ten to fifteen million nightly audience, agreed to put on a special five-minute news programme to cover Common Market issues and developments; the third and still more extraordinary feature of the media breakfast was who financed them. In

8

money terms the amount must have been trivial, and at the time it was assumed that the European Movement, under its director Ernest Wistrich, had met the bill. In fact, as only very recently has been discovered, the breakfasts were paid for by the IRD itself and their contribution hidden in the accounts of the European Movement.

The media breakfasts were a most important part of the total effort to shift opinion in the UK. The involvement of senior officials of the Foreign Office and senior executives of the BBC in a covert propaganda campaign was a disgraceful breach of the relevant codes of conduct affecting Crown servants and of the BBC's Charter obligations. The whole operation was a closely guarded secret. It was brought to an end, after the crucial October 1971 White Paper vote, only through the personal intervention of the Head of the civil service, Sir William Armstrong.

The operation was however penetrated and opened up by a distinguished academic and author, the late Uwe Kitzinger, himself an ardent pro-Marketeer, who documented these and other events in his *Diplomacy and Persuasion* as long ago as 1973. Further dimensions of the story were unfolded recently, by Larkin and Oliver in their *A Discreet Word: Britain's Secret Propaganda During the Cold War* (1998).

What these authors were able to make plain was that the media breakfasts were only one, though a most important component, in the whole pro-Market propaganda campaign. In particular, they were able to document in much greater detail the role played by Norman Reddaway and his IRD. His team were the authors of daily drafts of articles, and letters, signed as arranged by the IRD, by the Conservative MP, Sir Tufton Beamish and his pro-European friends, in the *Times* and other papers. Immediate rebuttal of anti-Market statements and allegations was just one of the facilities made available. The unit was in daily not just weekly, contact with the Today programme and News-at-Ten.

Geoffrey Rippon, Chancellor of the Duchy of Lancaster and Heath's Negotiator-in-Chief, was personally involved in all these activities, and so were his fellow ministers at the Foreign Office. Tony Royle, the Parliamentary Secretary at the Foreign Office, chaired a governmental co-ordinating committee to bring together the many different interests involved. What Larkin and Oliver were also able to discover, from the documents made available to them by Sir Richard Body, a strongly anti-Common Market Conservative MP, was the active involvement of the US Central Intelligence Agency (CIA) in promoting, covertly, the campaign for European Unity on the continent and in the UK as well.

The final confirmation of the truth of this whole extraordinary story came early in this year, on a Radio 4 half-hour programme, presented by Christopher Cook and broadcast on 3 February. In an interview with the long retired Norman Reddaway, shortly before he died, the facts of the IRD's involvement including the media breakfasts, the placing of pro-Market articles and letters drafted by his unit was duly confirmed. Cook also interviewed Geoffrey Tucker, Ernest Wistrich, and the Labour politicians Hattersley and Healey, as well as others directly involved.

A particularly repellent incident, first recounted in Kitzinger's original 1972 book, was that Trethowan had replaced Jack de Manio at the Today programme because he was alleged by a number of breakfasters to be anti-Common Market. This the BBC continues to deny. But not the least interesting of Cook's interrogations was with Roy Hattersley. In 1971 Hattersley, a Labour Front Bencher, was then as now an ardent Europhile. In his interview with Cook, Hattersley claimed that he had attended only one media breakfast because he said that some of his breakfast companions had urged Ian Trethowan 'to do something' about anti-European broadcasters and that 'I was so shocked that I decided I couldn't go again'. Roy Hattersley, in my experience, is

10

not easily shocked and one can't help therefore but give some credibility to what is alleged.

One further episode in this strange story must now be related – the extent of the CIA's involvement. US government policy had long been committed to promoting European unity, if possible with the UK as a member state. No doubt the CIA was tasked to assist with that enterprise and it appears to be the fact that the European movement, even in earlier years, was a recipient of CIA funds. With the votes of the 1975 referendum in doubt and the prospect of UK withdrawal, the CIA went far beyond its previous low-profile approaches. A new Head of Station in the UK, Cord Meyer Jnr, was appointed (a man with known federalist views) with the general remit to use American influence in favour of the Yes campaign.

Two very Anglophile CIA employees informed Sir Richard Body MP what was afoot and showed him documents of the CIA involvement with the European Movement. Hot stuff. Yet Body was unable to find a single British newspaper to publish the story or the documents. In the end Body was able to publish the story in *Time Out* – at that time still a small-circulation magazine and not one that carried weight with the establishment or public opinion.

This is a story which, once again, one would hesitate to reproduce without copper-bottomed guarantees of its authenticity. Such evidence however is now available. Dr Richard Aldrich of the Department of Politics at Nottingham University, while researching CIA activities in Europe, stumbled across an archive of CIA front organisations in Georgetown University, Washington. The documents revealed that, over the years, millions of dollars had been funnelled mainly into Europe but some into the UK, with relevant correspondence including letters from British MPs. Cord, appointed Head of Station in London only in 1975, departed in 1976, the special mission of helping to keep Britain in Europe accomplished.

My conclusion from all this is *not* that these covert and irregular activities were decisive in either the House of Commons vote in October 1971, or in the referendum decision in 1975. It is simply that the normal standards of political and public service behaviour, of ministers, MPs, broadcasters and civil servants collapsed and were abandoned when government and people were faced with what was and remains the greatest single issue in our post-war history.

There is, however, a vast area that falls between the totally unacceptable conduct just described and what is reasonable and responsible conduct by senior politicians in a democracy. Certain standards and self-disciplines in presentation are crucial. Quite properly, the ultimate sin in the House of Commons is for a Minister or Member to lie knowingly. Yes: but there is a vast range of verbal formulas that fall short of lying but which have intended effects, ranging from placing a favourable gloss on events to seriously misleading Parliament and the public. The nuances are important and the correct and honest choice of words is what largely distinguishes the good Minister from the bad. And there are too conventions that Ministers must observe: including maintaining the impartiality and objectivity of their own civil servants in presenting – and not withholding – information; and civil servants themselves must play by the rules, by their own codes of conduct.

Before citing some examples of serious ministerial deceit, I want as a plea in mitigation for other ministers involved to identify two particular difficulties that the European question posed and still poses for politicians and commentators – even when they are trying to be objective and fair. The first is the built-in ambiguity in the European Treaties of its supranational and intergovernmental characteristics, an ambiguity greatly, if temporarily, increased during General de Gaulle's ten-year period in power when he halted and nearly reversed the essential supranationalism of the Treaties: and second, the momentum for change built into the whole concept of 'ever closer union', with expanding membership, extending competence of the supranational institutions, with changing practices, new treaties and treaty amendments.

Let me cite some famous examples. During the 1975 Referendum Campaign, every elector was sent three documents: a statement of case by the No campaign, a similar statement by the Yes campaign and – odd when one thinks about it – a third statement, by the government, recommending a Yes vote.

The point I want to stress is this. The government's three-page document contained, among other things, two important assurances. First: 'There was a threat to employment in Britain from the movement in the Common Market towards an Economic and Monetary Union (EMU). This could have forced us to accept fixed exchange rates for the pound, restricting industrial growth and so putting jobs at risk. This threat has been removed.' And secondly: 'No important new policy can be decided in Brussels or anywhere else without the consent of a British Minister answerable to a British government and British Parliament ... the Minister representing Britain can veto any proposals for a new law or new tax if he considers it to be against British interest.'

Very reassuring. But both these statements, read today, are self-evidently untrue. The threat to employment posed by fixed exchange rates or an EMU, far from vanishing, is all too obviously present in the single currency, the European Central Bank and the Economic and Monetary Union. Similarly, the right of veto is now possessed by the UK and other member states in only a small area of the treaties – and under constant pressure of further contraction.

Governments very seldom make statements that they *know* to be false and, in particular, statements whose falsity can be publicly demonstrated. If for no other reason, the loss of credibility is too great. Why then did Wilson and the majority of his Cabinet agree to make these statements?

The answer is that, though those assertions could well have been challenged, they were not flagrantly false in 1975, the time when they were made. EMU, which was indeed on the Common Market agenda as early as 1972, was driven off it by the huge upheaval of the Arab oil shock the following year. And the belief that we could always veto what we disliked was a direct consequence, not of evaluating the content of the Treaties, but of de Gaulle's 'empty chair' policy in the Council of Ministers (the French decision not to attend any EC meetings). This had led to the so-called Luxembourg Compromise in 1966, i.e. the agreement to differ, on the French claim that where a vital national interest was involved it could not be over-ridden.

Additionally there was an element of self-deception. Wilson hoped that he was right because he was opposed both to EMU and to majority voting in the EC. (Subsequent events have of course destroyed the Luxembourg Compromise – though politicians still, ignorantly or dishonestly, make reference to it.)

The other great difficulty – apart from the fact that the Treaties seem to be almost deliberately incomprehensible – that the European Union poses, is the changes produced by its own momentum and enlargement. With the aim of 'ever-closer union' there are few boundaries in state policy and law or in geographical extent that can check its growth and expansion. So the game is constantly changing – like the various official titles or disguises of the organisation itself: the Common Market, the EEC, the EC, the European Union – what it was thirty, twenty, or ten years ago is not necessarily what it is today.

Inevitably politicians can make statements that are more or less true when they make them, but which they have good reason to believe – often with their own approval – will become false in the near future. Central to all this is the driving purpose of further integration and the ultimate creation of a European state.

Introduction

I must turn now to the most serious offence – deception. In the practice of the deliberate half-truth Ted Heath is, regrettably, a main offender. Of course Ted Heath knew the political as well as the economic implications of joining the European Economic Community. He learned what it was about and what it was programmed to become in the prolonged negotiations of 1961-3, which he led, and still more when, as Prime Minister, he master-minded the 'successful' break-in to membership with the Treaty of Accession and the 1972 European Communities Act. Ted Heath not only knew. He actively willed its further development.

It is against this background of knowledge and commitment that we have to judge his now famous pronouncements on joining Europe.

The 1970 Election pledge simply 'to negotiate, no more and no less' and to join only with 'the full-hearted consent of the British people' are mere peccadilloes. Much more serious was the statement in the October 1971 White Paper that in membership 'there is no question of any erosion of essential national sovereignty' – and his endlessly repeated assertions that the UK was only 'pooling sovereignty' when it was in fact subjecting itself to the supremacy of Community Law, to decisions taken by qualified majority vote and to European Court of Justice rulings.

Heath had in fact been informed much earlier as to the meaning of the Treaties. At the start of the first Macmillan application in 1961 when Heath was the Cabinet's principal negotiator, he had written on the very matter to his colleague the Lord Chancellor, then Lord Kilmuir (who was himself a keen supporter of British membership). In response, Kilmuir made a lengthy and considered response covering the impact of the UK signing of the European treaties on Parliament, on the UK's treaty-making powers and on the independence of our courts of law.

Kilmuir concluded: 'I must emphasise that in my view the surrender of sovereignty involved are serious ones ... I am sure that it would be a great mistake to under-estimate the force of the objections to them. But these objections ought to be brought out into the open now …'

Clear enough in 1961. Since then, General de Gaulle had intervened in 1966 with the 'Luxembourg Compromise'. But, unlike Harold Wilson, there is no reason to believe that Heath himself had accepted the authority – let alone the desirability – of the Gaullist assertion of the right to veto, as stated in the Compromise. True, Heath can point to occasions when he made clear that in joining the European Community we were joining something that aimed way beyond a free trade area surrounded by a common external tariff. But these extra dimensions were *sotto voce* mutterings against his trumpeting statements that we were joining a Common Market, with the prospects of great benefit to British traders and to Britain's economic prosperity.

Once Parliament had accepted the Treaty of Accession and passed the European Communities' Act that brought it into effect, Heath and his new partners in Europe were able to be more open about their plans and projects. In the second half of 1972, with France in the Chair of the EC's rotating six-month Presidency, Pompidou called a special conference in Paris, the first Meeting of Heads of State or governments of the member states, to welcome the newcomers – the UK, Eire and Denmark, and to launch the next phase of integration. As the communiqué put it, and as Heath proudly restated it in the House of Commons on 23 October 1972, the Heads of Government had 'affirmed their intention to transform the whole complex of their relationships into a European Union by the end of the decade'.

That promised transformation of 'the whole complex of their relationships into a European Union' by 1980 did not in fact occur. Indeed, it was not until 1991, with the Treaty of Maastricht, that the goal of European Union and its vastly extended content was reached. But Heath knew in 1972 what were the objectives and likely content.

He decided, however, not to tell Parliament and the people what they were. By this deliberate refusal to state what he knew to be true about the European Communities's plans and by withholding relevant information from the public, Heath set a precedent for ministerial handling of European affairs that many have followed since.

I shall end my account with two contemporary examples of the behaviour of New Labour since its election to power in May 1997. Among Gordon Brown's first pronouncements as Chancellor of the Exchequer was a two-year freeze on public expenditure to the totals announced by his Conservative predecessor, Kenneth Clarke. Although this astonishing commitment had been made public in January 1997 and was included in Labour's March manifesto; it was neither mentioned in the July 1996 pre-election draft manifesto, nor debated/approved by party members. A key decision had been made by Gordon Brown without collective discussion or consultation; except with Tony Blair.

Of course, this decision has been explained as deliberate shock treatment, to convince everyone in Britain and in the outside world that there was no danger whatever to vested interests and the maintenance of the status quo from New Labour; that New Labour was really 'new' and had turned its back upon the wicked 'tax and spend' policies of its Old Labour predecessors; that, in personal terms, here was an Iron Chancellor who, come what may and regardless of what his Party members and voters expected, was determined to take no risk with the economy – a man whose middle name was Prudent.

All of this is persuasive. But there was another influential factor. The previous government of John Major and Gordon Brown's predecessor as Chancellor, Ken Clarke, had received each year since 1994 a Decision made by the European Council of Ministers informing them that the UK had been found to be running 'an excessive deficit', well above the 3 per cent of GDP borrowing limit and in breach of their treaty commitments not to do so when signing up to the second phase of the Economic and Monetary Union (EMU).

Of course, John Major in government had no wish to draw attention to this Council of Ministers' decision. Nor, significantly, did the Labour Front Bench, normally in Opposition only too eager to expose and censure the failure of Tory economic policies. Meanwhile Kenneth Clarke showed his readiness to comply with European instructions and produced successive budgets based upon measures first to reduce the gap and then to close it.

The task was still incomplete when the May 1997 Election put Brown in Clarke's place at the Treasury. Only too anxious to show himself to be 'a good European', as well as an Iron Chancellor, Brown accepted without demur the Council of Ministers' recommendation of 1996 and its successor in 1997, and their decision that the UK's 'excessive deficit' still remained and that it had to be corrected. He also accepted that 'a further reduction of the government's deficit is necessary in view of the objectives of the Stability and Growth Pact'. The full meaning of the reference to the 'further reduction' remains unclear, but it certainly looks as though the European Council's commitment now embraces not merely an annual borrowing ceiling of 3 per cent of GDP but a 'balanced budget' over what the European Commission and Council judge to be the span of years that form the economic cycle.

On all this, the government has been coyness itself. True there is a provision in the treaty that requires the Council of Ministers, when making these extremely sensitive decisions concerning the economic policy of a member state, itself not to publicise its recommendations – providing that its recommendations, or rather instructions, are obeyed. That, after all, is a minimum requirement. Otherwise an adverse decision, made public, might well lead to a loss of confidence in a country's economy and to a flight from its currency.

But it has been kept secret not just by the European Council but also by the UK government, even when the deficit problem ceased to exist. It has been kept secret by the government – and by its predecessor – because these recommendations confirm the surrender of the independence of our own Chancellor of the Exchequer, even in matters of budgetary finance, to an unelected outside agency.

I have myself tried to tease the government into the open on this matter. The last response, a written answer from a Minister in the Lords, about excess deficits produced the following:

> Under protocol 25 of the EC Treaty (ex protocol 11) the UK is not legally bound to avoid running an excess deficit. The European Council of Finance Ministers has no power to enforce recommendations made under Article 104(7) on the UK. But the UK is obliged under Article 116(4) to 'endeavour to avoid excessive government deficits'.

I am not a lawyer but a bit of familiar legal jargon keeps running through my head: *verbum veritas sed suggestio falsi* – true words but false or disguised meanings. Formal powers of the EC to direct and command a future Chancellor of the Exchequer to close or reduce his excess deficits – and to punish him if he refuses – will only operate in the third phase of EMU, if and when we join the single currency. Meanwhile in the second phase of EMU where we are now, the Council can only make 'recommendations' which, if a UK government rejects them, can then be made public knowledge with all the damaging market turmoil that is likely to ensue.

In fact, New Labour's obeisance before the European Council went well beyond the promise to maintain the public spending totals of their predecessors. Gordon Brown presented a new convergence programme in September 1997, stating his two strict rules for future conduct. In the words of the EC document which I am reading as I write, 'borrowing will be limited to covering investment requirements over the cycle; and Government debt will be held stable and at a prudent level in terms of its ratio to GDP'.

In response to this, the Council 'welcomed the government's commitment to sound finances' and further recommended that: 'The UK Government strictly implements its budgetary policy and that it achieves a Government out-turn for 1998 and 1999 and subsequent years that is close to balance when due allowance is made for the economy's cyclical position'.

For good measure, the Council concluded by stressing to the errant UK in 1997 'the importance of maintaining a rigorous control of public expenditure as has featured in budget commitments in recent years'. The Health Service may well have had to wait and so have other public sector expenditure programmes but 'the excess deficit' disappeared and the UK was formally discharged by the Council on 18 November 1998.

All this gives too an explanation – not exactly volunteered – by the Chancellor of the policy volte face on privatisation and his enthusiastic embrace of the private finance initiative. Selling off public assets obviously reduces the public sector borrowing requirement. And the great advantage of the public finance initiative and various other partnership schemes is that they allow for heavy expenditure on public assets – new hospitals, new schools, air traffic control, computer systems – previously paid by governments out of taxation or borrowing, now to be financed and owned by private industry and leased or rented to the government.

In the longer term, it may cost the government more – figures suggest considerably more – but in the short term such expenditures count much less against the EC's controlled and defined borrowing requirement. It is this that explains – although the government has yet to admit it – why facilities as sensitive as the air traffic control computer system at our airports are now to be partially privatised in a so-called public-private partnership (PPP) and placed under private management in spite of the overriding importance of safety in all air control operations. And it is this that explains the dangerous project of privatising British Nuclear Fuels with its even more safety-sensitive management issues, affecting the processing of uranium and plutonium, its heavily guarded supply to customers and the deposit of its dangerous, long-life wastes.

I wish that the story of deception and the hidden truth could end here. But there is a final chapter that has to be told. Tony Blair is of course the most genuine and ardent European integrationist Prime Minister we have had since Ted Heath – and Gordon Brown, in spite of deliberately spun rumours to the contrary, is not far behind in dedication. This may help to explain but it certainly does not excuse the fundamental dishonesty of New Labour's whole approach to the single currency and to the European Union.

I have pondered and hesitated over that word, dishonesty. In particular I have toyed with the formula: 'An exceptional capacity for self-deception'. But, regretfully, it would be dishonest to adopt it. In brief, Blair and Brown know very well that, important for the economy as the single currency project is or may be, its major significance is not in the area of economics at all. It lies above all in politics and most obviously in the great step that a single currency is bound to take towards a European political union, a European State. Together they wrote or approved in the early months of 1997 Labour's Manifesto and they jointly agreed these defining words: 'Our vision of Europe is of an alliance of independent nations choosing to co-operate to achieve goals they cannot achieve alone.'

But frankly, on the evidence, that is incredible. Those are the words that one would write in describing any treaty of which we are a signatory – NATO, the Non-Proliferation Treaty, the OEEC, the World Trade Organisation and countless others. What is incontrovertibly special about the European Union and its treaty base is precisely its supranationalism, its declared purpose of 'ever closer union' and its unique institutions that set it apart from all others. The words in Labour's Manifesto are chosen to deceive simply because the authors know that the electors, to whom the manifesto is addressed, do not want to be integrated into a European Union – do not want to lose their birthright of democracy and self-government.

The following words in the manifesto, 'We oppose a European Federal Super State', deserve more serious consideration if only because the ultimate shape of the European Union, federal or central, with the precise delineation of what powers and decisions should be taken at the Union level and what should be left to the nation states, has yet to be finally determined.

But one has only to look at the headings of the Maastricht and Amsterdam Treaties – let alone the agenda of the new Inter-Governmental Conference (IGC) to prepare for the European Union's enlargement – to understand that the integration project is on the march in every area of state activity. And New Labour wants to be in the van: at the heart of Europe, giving leadership, sponsoring the new European defence initiative, among others.

What is so extraordinary is that the pretence of British politicians that Europe is not about political union is now openly contradicted by virtually all our European neighbours. In earlier decades, while the federal purpose was always and clearly there, federalists them-selves, with the clear guidance of their leader Jean Monnet, agreed that it would be imprudent to constantly stress this objective – that it was better to adopt tactics of softly, softly and of incremental change. But the signing of the Maastricht Treaty and the subsequent May 1998 agreement to launch the single currency on 1 January 1999, seems to have unbuttoned continental lips and released statements of purpose and intent that, previously, prudence about the feelings of their own electors – and of the reluctant British voter as well – had constrained.

It would be tedious to quote them all, but here is just a sample of what they have been saying. Gonzales, former Spanish Prime Minister, speaking shortly after the decision of the eleven to join the euro asserted that: 'The Single Currency is the greatest abandonment of sovereignty since the foundation of the European Community ... we need this United Europe ... we must never forget the euro is an instrument for this project'. The voice of Belgium in the person of its then Prime Minister Jean Luc Dehaene claimed that 'monetary union is the motor of European integration'. The then Italian Finance Minister, now President Carlo Ciampi, was scarcely less forthcoming when he said: 'I don't think we will have a Federal government but something between a Federal State and a Federation of States'.

It is the German leaders who have been most open about what has been achieved, its significance, and what they see as the next European goals. Kohl himself, Chancellor until 1998 and the longest serving European leader, gave this judgement on the Maastricht Treaty: 'In Maastricht we laid the foundation stone for the completion of the European Union. The European Union Treaty introduces a new and decisive stage in the process of European union which within a few years will lead to the creation of what the founding fathers of modern Europe dreamed after the last war: the United States of Europe.'

And Kohl's successors in the SDP-Green Coalition government have been equally clear. Their first Finance Minister, Oskar Lafontaine, openly stated that 'the United States of Europe has been the aim of the SDP all along'. His successor, the present incumbent, the less flamboyant Hans Eichel, wrote in January 1999: 'We will now strive towards a political unification ... EMU will not be enough ... why do we still need national armies? One European army is enough.' Fischer, his Foreign Minister colleague said shortly after the coalition election victory in a speech on 12 January 1999: 'For the first time in the history of the European integration process ... an important part of national sovereignty, to wit monetary sovereignty, has passed over to a European institution ... the introduction of a common currency is not primarily an economic but rather a sovereign and thus eminently political act.' And, if that wasn't enough, in an earlier speech on 26 November 1998 he said: 'Transforming a European Union into a single state with one army, one constitution and one foreign policy is the critical challenge of the age.'

When on the specific question of the single currency the President of the Bundesbank Hans Tietmeyer predicts that 'the European currency will lead to member nations transferring their sovereignty over financial and wage policies as well as in monetary affairs. It is an illusion to think that states can hold on to their autonomy over taxation policies' – and when the President of the new European Central Bank Wim Duisenberg publicly asserts 'the process of Monetary Union goes hand in hand, with political integration and ultimately political union' and last, but not least, when Duisenberg also asserts 'EMU is and always was meant to be a stepping stone on the way to a United Europe' – how can Tony Blair and Gordon Brown, as honourable men, continue to claim that the single currency is simply about an assessment of economic advantage and continue to deny that it has as well a vast significance for national independence and for European political union?

Against these statements, none of which has led to protests or contradictions by any other member state, how can the British Prime Minister, the Foreign Secretary, the Chancellor and others pretend that this political intent is just rhetoric, to be dismissed from serious discussion as no more than eurosceptic hysteria?

Tony Blair himself has volunteered in one of his many articles in the *Sun* these words: 'New Labour will have no truck with the European superstate and if there are those in Europe who want a federal superstate, we would refuse to go along'. How then can he justify his own active support at European Heads of Government Councils for the appointment of Signor Prodi in 1999, an open federalist, as the new President of the European Commission – the most powerful post in the European Union?

As though to remove any possible doubt about the direction and commitment of the new Commission's President, in between his nomination and endorsement, Prodi spoke these words: 'The euro was a decision that completely changed the nature of the nation states. The pillars of the nation state are the sword and currency and we changed that.' As for the future: 'The real goal is to draw on the consequences of the single currency and create a political Europe'. And a few months later he was openly calling for a Common European Army as 'the logical next step'.

So: one is left with the question, who is telling the truth about the European Union, the single currency and its further ambitions? Is it the British government or virtually all its 'partners' in Europe?

Does it matter? Unfortunately, yes. It matters not least to the quality and standards of our own public life, to the maintenance of open and honest discourse between opposing judgements of where the national interest lies. Above all, if democracy itself is to endure, it does demand minimum standards of integrity in the presentation of both fact and argument by its principal players.

The one thing on which Europhiles and Eurosceptics agree is that the decision on the single currency is the most significant that we have been asked to make in these post-war years. Since that very importance has been recognised in the pledge made by government and opposition to hold a referendum so that the decision will have the direct authority of people as well as Parliament, it is essential that the campaign is conducted honestly, that the rival opinions are given equal opportunity to be heard and that the facts, where they are relevant, are properly presented.

This time, the referendum will take place in very different circumstances from those in 1975. The national press is more or less evenly divided. The BBC knows that its past misdeeds have been discovered and that it will next time be closely monitored as to its impartiality. The Confederation of British Industry is clearly tilted into the Yes camp but much of business, including such organisations as the Institute of Directors and the Small Business Federation, are hostile. Between them, the Neill Committee and the government's response have devised rules of conduct for future referendums which will ban the 1975 two-to-one advantage, impose a ceiling on campaign expenditure and limit contributions to authorised protagonists. Also, with public opinion strongly and now for a substantial period of time in favour of keeping the pound sterling, the prospects here too are different And in the argument itself, the Nos have good grounds for their belief that theirs is by far the stronger case.

So, can we now relax? We would be foolish to do so for three reasons. First, it has to be accepted, however reluctantly, that part of our governing elite and the people who work with and for them, are now servants of the European federal dream. Their motive is invariably idealistic but – not unlike dedicated Marxist fellow travellers of the Soviet Union, some of whom became agents and apologists – there are few self-imposed limits on their personal conduct and political behaviour that these Europhiles are prepared to accept. The cause is all.

That of course describes only the most extreme Europhiles and nation-state haters. But the milder, less fanatical, European fellow travellers are now a formidable force in British government and among those who handle and decide the affairs of our nation. There will be no hesitation in using every conceivable opportunity to sway opinion – either to denigrate the personnel and the arguments of the No campaign or, more promisingly, to frighten and confuse the voting public. Scaremongering about jobs is now clearly established as a potential trump card in the debate. Certainly we must expect the government machine and pro-European commercial and professional organisations to come together to launch vigorous Yes propaganda campaigns.

The second reason for staying on guard is the clear danger, in spite of the Neill Committee-government legislative changes to regulate expenditures during referendums and elections, that the government will not be able to keep out of the UK money from European companies who trade with Britain. While the new legislation prohibits foreigners and foreign corporations from pouring money into UK political parties and UK elections, the European Court of Justice has decided that European companies are not foreign and that, so long as they conduct some trade with the UK, they cannot be prevented from spending campaign money in this country.

The implications of this for the integrity of our politics and for our future independence are indeed enormous. And when one considers that the European Union political establishment and European corporations both ardently want to rope the UK into the single currency and that to do so a majority of the British people have to be persuaded in a referendum campaign, the temptation and motivation for massive European financial intervention is self evident.

The third reason why we cannot rest is directly connected with the previous two: the known fact of widespread corrupt practices in European politics. This is not the place to explore the behaviour of the European Commission and its lack of accountability to that feeble Assembly, the European Parliament. But it is the moment to reflect on the recent exposures that have disgraced former Chancellor Kohl. At the centre of the charges against him and his ruling CDU Party is the acceptance of unauthorised monies from varying sources including the French government, through the direct agency of President Mitterand. The reason for the transfer of funds was not because Kohl and Mitterand were in the usual sense 'corrupt' (i.e. gaining for themselves financial advantage) but because, as strong Europeans, they had convinced themselves that their continued partnership in government was essential to further the European cause: that Kohl's CDU must be helped to win the first general election to be held in a United Germany.

There is little doubt that cross-border money for the European cause has flowed to other European countries including, almost certainly, Italy. Former Prime Minister Bettino Craxi, the Italian negotiator of the Maastricht Treaty, was forced to spend the last years of his life in exile in Tunisia, following charges of serious electoral malpractice when in office in Italy. In a positive tribute to his father, and to his motivation, his son Vittorio Craxi had this to say: 'There is a huge difference between taking money in exchange for favours and taking money for one's political movement, to build political stability.' 'Kohl, Mitterand and Craxi not only built Europe, they also fought to resolve regional conflicts and bring peace to areas such as the Middle East. They made the world safer for all of us.'

What to do? Totally secure defences in the UK are almost impossible to erect. But there is one demand on our government by our people that has to be met, whatever the difficulties, whatever the treaty law and the European Court of Justice may say, it is this: 'You must not permit European money, whether from individuals, corporations or European Union institutions to enter this country for the purpose of influencing/corrupting our political parties and the votes to be cast in our elections and referendums.'

* I prefer 'Euro-realist' and wholly reject 'Europhobe'.

Part I

1

Post-War Europe

France, Britain and a Cage for Germany

The important story of Britain and Europe is a story that long ante-
dates the formation of the European Communities in the 1950s. The
struggles of the UK against the dominant continental powers of
Spain, France and Germany occupy a large part of the last four
centuries of European history – with the UK generally successful in
opposing the attempts of the leading continental power of the time
to achieve hegemony in Europe itself and supremacy in the struggle
for overseas territories in the New Worlds of the Americas and elsewhere. However, for reasons which will soon become clear, my
chosen starting point is the 1945 Potsdam conference.

The Potsdam Conference was attended by the heads of government
of the UK, the USA and USSR in that small East German town. There
they met in the Cecilienhof Palace, residence of the former German
Crown Prince, in mid-July, some eight weeks after the unconditional
surrender of the German armed forces on 11 May. This was the first
post-war conference of the victorious Allies, and the future of occupied Germany, of war-torn Europe, the future prosecution of the war
against Japan and the final structure of the United Nations were on
the agenda, along with a host of immediate problems for managing a
continent in ruins and faced with the collapse of civil order.

Potsdam marks one of the great turning points in twentieth-
century history. For it was at Potsdam that, in addition to the matters

already listed, that the new American President, Harry Truman, was to inform his po-faced but deeply concerned colleague, Joseph Stalin, the Soviet dictator, that the US had now mastered and possessed a new and deadly weapon, the atomic bomb. The nuclear age dawned.

And it was at Potsdam too that the workings of British democracy must have surprised, if not shocked, Stalin almost as much as the news of the American monopoly of nuclear weapons: the defeat of Winston Churchill in the British general election and his replacement at the Conference itself by his former deputy, Clement Attlee. The resulting upheaval in Britain's internal policies was not reflected however in Britain's external relations – at least with the Soviet Union. 'Left did not speak to Left' with any more sympathy and understanding of the Soviet Union through the mouths of Attlee and Bevin than had been shown by Churchill and Eden during the earlier post-war years.

For all these reasons, Potsdam was a memorable occasion. But there was another feature – at the time hardly noticed – of that Potsdam Conference that deserves special emphasis for its inherent importance. *France was not there.* Certainly, that was not Churchill's fault. He had fought like a tiger at the last war-time conference of the Big Three at Yalta in February 1945 to press the French case not only for permanent membership of the Security Council of the United Nations, with its veto-carrying power, but for France to be awarded a separate zone of occupation when Germany was defeated, and a seat on the Four Power Control Commission to be set up in Berlin. Churchill pressed the French claim against the strong resistance of both the Soviet Union and the United States, still represented by the ailing Roosevelt who was virulently hostile to France's General de Gaulle. In spite of that formidable combination, Churchill won.

But de Gaulle was not a man to show gratitude. As the head of state in liberated France since allied troops (with the French carefully positioned in the lead) re-occupied Paris in October 1944, he bitterly resented the absence of France from the Potsdam Conference. This mattered in immediate, practical terms because, Churchill having won for him one of the four places in the government of occupied Germany, nothing agreed at Potsdam affecting Germany could in fact be implemented without French agreement – and the French, with their ambition to separate the Ruhr permanently from Germany, had a strong special interest of their own. But the absence of France mattered, as we shall see, much more fundamentally than in debates about the future government and composition of occupied Germany.

This marked the starting point of a divergence between Britain and France that was to dominate and shape the development of Western Europe and of Britain's increasingly difficult relationships with her continental neighbours: a divergence that has continued and increased throughout the past half-century and which remains a major item on the British national agenda today.

For while the history of this past half-century in Europe reflects the impact of many other internal and external forces, a central and abiding theme has been the tug-of-war between France and Britain to reshape the continent to achieve their own interests and priorities. For France – and not just for de Gaulle who stood down in late 1946 to be recalled twelve years later, but for his successors on both occasions as well – the restoration of French power and influence in Europe and in world affairs was the first of their policy priorities. Their second one, and intimately bound up with the first, was the search for a permanent solution to the German threat.

No one with any knowledge of European history can be surprised that these should be the overriding determinants of French policy. In three quarters of a century, France had endured the defeat and humiliation of the 1870 Franco/Prussian war; the terrible blood-letting of 1914–18, a war fought throughout on French (and Belgian) soil; and, most terrible of all, the defeat and occupation by the armies of Hitler's Germany in 1940; the shame of occupation, of collabora-

33

tion, of Vichy's puppet governments and the physical destruction caused first by the German invasion then, four years later, by the Anglo-American liberation, with France a battlefield from the Normandy beaches to the River Rhine. The neighbour from hell indeed.

For Britain, while feeling strong sympathy for the French determination to 'solve' the German problem, the post-war priorities were inevitably different. First and foremost, at Potsdam, the Second World War had yet to be won. Vast British and Commonwealth armed forces were still committed in the struggle for Burma and a great sea-borne invasion of the Malaysian peninsula was shortly to be launched. Further, the Soviet Union had yet to enter the war against Japan and while the coming availability of the atom bomb was known to British leaders, its deadly destructiveness was not yet appreciated. Maintaining the 'Grand Alliance' with the Soviet Union was therefore of great military importance, since the Japanese armies were still undefeated. Second, British post-war strategy was heavily involved in maintaining security while successfully disengaging its rule from many British occupied areas of the world outside Europe, including the Middle East and the Indian subcontinent. Then, from 1947 onwards, in facing the new challenge of Soviet power in Europe itself, there was the over-riding need to persuade the Americans to a halt and reverse their withdrawal from the European Continent.

But, while the priorities of France and Britain were clearly, indeed inevitably different, there was, when objectively appraised, no inherent reason why the two neighbour states should find themselves so often and so seriously opposed.

The problem arose not so much from the pursuit of the French goal of removing the German threat as from their method of doing so. From 1950 onwards France was to sponsor the creation of supranational institutions, with ever-widening scope and ever-increasing embrace, of which the European Coal and Steel Community provided the first and shaping frame. It was this that enabled France not merely to advance its own national interest and to seek the revival of its own power and status but also to harness, when that proved to be the more effective way, the drive and idealism of European federalism to construct ever-stronger and more complex cages for the containment of German power.

The history of Britain and Europe in the past half century cannot be understood without recognition of this persistent and dynamic thrust in French policy. The establishment of supranational institutions inevitably posed real and abiding problems for the UK. Less important, but not to be ignored, was the associated thrust of France to revive her great power role and in particular to challenge and reduce the dominating influence on European affairs of the Anglo-Saxons – of the United States certainly but of the British as well, both because of the UK's intimacy with the US and because of our greater vulnerability.

The unfolding of these French initiatives in Europe in the years after Potsdam was played out alongside – and in public attention, largely overshadowed by – the much more dramatic and dangerous events that ended the wartime Grand Alliance; events which led, less than two years after the defeat of Germany, to the Cold War between the Soviet Union and the West that was to divide Europe and much of the world for nearly fifty years. The course of the Cold War itself was on many occasions to connect with the often contending aims of British, American, French and German policy in Europe.

In the immediate post-war period Britain could have hardly been more helpful and understanding of the anxieties of her French neighbour. The first treaty that Britain signed in post-war Europe was the Anglo-French Treaty of Dunkirk in 1946, which promised unconditional UK aid to France if France were again to face a German attack. This was followed in March 1948 by the Brussels Treaty, embracing the three Benelux countries along with France and Britain in pledges of mutual support, specifically if attacked by Germany – and unusually, in such a treaty, substantial provisions for economic co-operation as well.

For the British, over-extended and near-exhausted as they were, other priorities had also to be pursued. First and foremost, as American 'lease-lend' arrangements with the UK abruptly ceased within weeks of the Japanese surrender and as the amount and terms of the American Loan were clearly both insufficient and too harsh, and as America pressed forward with early demobilisation and 'bringing the boys back home', the aim had to be to keep America in Europe: not just to avert the economic disaster which, without US help, would certainly have ensued but to bring a necessary counterweight into play against the formidable Soviet armed presence, its aggressive diplomacy and the activities throughout Western Europe and the world of the Soviet-linked communist parties.

It was therefore with enthusiasm that Foreign Secretary Bevin welcomed Secretary of State George Marshall's Harvard speech of June 1947 and turned his words into the practical economic revival programmes of the 'Marshall Aid'. Similarly, with vast relief, the British heard the enunciation in 1948 of the Truman Doctrine and in 1949 the vast reinforcement of its own Brussels Treaty attempt to improve security in Western Europe with the signing of the North Atlantic Treaty (NATO), pledging the forces of the United States and Canada to the collective defence of Europe. The New World had indeed come to the rescue of the Old.

Nor was Britain unmindful of the hopeful political forces at work on the continent: the genuine and widespread desire, going beyond the Franco/German special problem, to create Europe-wide institutions to help achieve a more secure and peaceful continent for the future. The British government itself gave official blessing to these moves, specifically in support of the Council of Europe, established in 1949, open to all European countries and soon to spawn its independent Court of Human Rights.

But the largest British contribution in this area came, not from the government but from the Leader of the Opposition, Winston Churchill. In a speech of truly remarkable wisdom and generosity, as early as September 1946, delivered in Zurich, Churchill was calling for 'the recreation of the European family', for an act of 'oblivion against all the crimes and follies of the past' and for a 'partnership between France and Germany' – and, as the first practical step, the formation of a Council of Europe.

Less than two years later, at the Congress of Europe in the Hague in May 1948, before what must have been the largest audience of European political leaders and other notables ever assembled, Churchill was once again preaching European unity, something close to a United States of Europe, with the immediate return of Italy to 'her full place in the comity of nations' and above all for the victor nations 'to take Germany by the hand and lead her back into the European family'.

In May 1949, the Council of Europe was formally established with the openly-federalist but experienced and realistic Spaak, the former Belgian Foreign Minister, as its first President. It possessed both a Council of Ministers and a Consultative Assembly and its initial membership included Britain, France, the Benelux Countries and Italy together with Eire and the Scandinavians. At the August meeting, Churchill spoke and called for the admission of Germany to the Council.

No one seriously considering this early post-war history can doubt the contribution that Britain made to the revival, indeed survival, of her continental neighbours; its magnanimity in victory to the defeated enemy; its generous vision for the future; its stoical endurance of continued austerity at home, nevermore vividly illustrated than in the UK government decision in the winter of 1946 to introduce bread rationing for its own people to help avoid near-starvation in the British zone of occupied Germany.

In spite of all this, the French sense of insecurity in relation to its German neighbour was not to be appeased. Germany, in spite of the burdens of allied occupation, reparation payments and, in the Soviet zone of East Germany, the wholesale stripping and deportation of industrial assets, was showing by 1948 early signs of economic recovery. In particular, before the end of 1949, it was clear that German steel production, limited by Allied decrees as much as by wartime and post-war damage, would soon have to be raised from 11 to 14 million tons – at American insistence – to a level that would outstrip that of France itself.

It was at this juncture that fate provided for France the man and the plan. Jean Monnet, lifelong federalist and most experienced industrialist and diplomat in the service of France, was then head of the renowned Commissariat de Plan. He wrote to his old friend, Foreign Minister Robert Schuman and to Prime Minister George Bidault, outlining his solution: to abandon separate national control of the coal and steel industries of Germany and France, together with those of Italy and the Benelux countries; to place the whole under the directorship and control of a newly-created body, an independent supranational High Authority; and to attach to it both a Council of Ministers of the Six countries and a Parliamentary Assembly.

As Monnet makes abundantly clear in his memoirs, the immediate purpose was to contain German industrial power and in particular to bring under supranational control the two great industries. 'Coal and steel were at once the key to economic power and the raw materials for forging weapons of war. This double role gave them immense symbolic significance ... comparable at that time to that of nuclear energy today.'

And Monnet was equally frank about its larger purpose. By forging this solid link between above all France and Germany, but with the other four countries as well, 'the way would be wide open for further collective action, and a great example would be given to the other nations of Europe'.

And so it was to be. Further collective action did follow and in five years, the Rome Treaty itself was to be signed. The French judged, correctly, that this emerging Coal and Steel Community (ECSC) as an organisation that the British in 1950 would not wish to join, not only because of its unmistakably supranational control provisions but because, having just nationalised Britain's own massive coal industry and with the nationalisation of steel shortly to be placed on the statute book, any such measure would have been strongly resisted not only in the House of Commons but in the many coal and steel communities up and down the land. What Monnet and Schuman feared however was that, while the UK would not wish to join, it would also actively oppose the others who wished to go ahead. The French therefore organised a manoeuvre which inevitably led to allegations of bad faith from the British side. The Schuman proposals were prepared in elaborate secrecy – but made known, exceptionally, to the United States Under Secretary of State, Dean Acheson, who happened to be in Paris on the eve of its public announcement, and who was therefore made privy to the French plan. Adenauer, the German Chancellor, was personally briefed and German acquiescence obtained, along with the consent of the Italians and the Benelux countries.

The plan was published the very day that a scheduled meeting of Foreign Ministers was held in London on 11 May 1950. Bevin was furious. Not so much because of the content of the proposals themselves – which UK officials at once began to examine seriously – as for the deception, which certainly did undermine trust between Britain and France and, as Acheson was acutely aware, with the United States as well. Nor were matters helped when, three weeks later, while the UK was still studying and probing with Paris the draft

ECSC proposals, the French government despatched an ultimatum to London on 1 June, giving the UK government until 8 pm that day to accept or reject the Schuman plan.

Extraordinary conduct. But it was indicative of the enormous importance that the French attached to what they saw as the strongest guarantee yet devised against the possible revival of Germany's ability to wage war.

And it worked. Britain, predictably, stayed out – although establishing later a liaison mission at the ECSC's Luxembourg headquarters. And Monnet's hope that it would 'open wide' the gates for creating similar supranational initiatives was soon to be realised.

Not for the last time in the UK/France/Europe story, events in the Cold War were to provide new pressures and new opportunities for French-led initiatives in Europe. In June 1950, in a period of already considerable East-West tension, the armies of Communist North Korea were launched across the 38th Parallel into the South. The US, the UK and other nations were immediately involved in armed conflict in the Korean peninsula. But North Korea could not, it was virtually everywhere agreed, have embarked upon so dangerous an exploit without the knowledge, equipment and approval of its Soviet neighbour. Was this therefore the prelude to a deliberately provoked incident, followed by a major assault on Germany and Western Europe?

Meeting in Lisbon, the NATO Council agreed to the formation of a collective defence force in Western Europe of no less than fifty divisions – the Labour government, among others, initiating a massive rearmament programme. But the crucial decision was about Germany. The fifty divisions simply couldn't be assembled without a large contribution from Germany itself. It was this that faced the whole of Europe with its most difficult post-war decision: whether or not to place arms again, only five years after her final defeat, in the hands of the nation that had conquered Europe and reduced its people to misery and despair.

For France the problem was indeed appalling. But the solution they volunteered was one largely inspired by the Schuman plan. In a few months of hectic diplomacy, the French created detailed proposals for a European Defence Community and for a European army in which the ECSC Six, including of course Germany, would contribute all their armed forces. There would be a supranational command structure and forces would be integrated and mixed down to battalion strengths. Article 1 of the treaty says it all: the Six set up among themselves 'a European defence community, supranational in character, comprising common institutions, Common Armed Forces and a common budget.' There were to be no other armed forces – except those needed outside Europe (mainly by France) in colonial territories. France quickly obtained the agreement of Germany and Italy and the Benelux countries, who all signed the Treaty of Paris in May 1952. The UK was not a member but promptly negotiated an Association Agreement.

All that was needed was the ratification of the treaty by the French Assembly. But, in an astonishing failure of nerve in the face of continued widespread hostility among French Parliamentarians and public to the rearmament of Germany in any form and to the placing of French armed forces under supranational control, the newly-formed government of Pierre Mendes-France, funked the issue. It declined to give government backing either for or against the treaty and put before the Assembly only a procedural motion that needed to be passed before the treaty itself could be considered and voted upon.

The procedural vote was lost: and so, for the first but not the last time, was the French-inspired European Army and Defence Community. Once again the British, ever sensitive to French anxieties about Germany, came to the rescue with Eden's historic commitment in the rapidly constructed London Treaty to the defence of France and Western Europe not just in general treaty pledges but in the new firm commitment to station four British divisions with supporting tactical airforces on the continent of Europe until the year 2025 – and not to withdraw them without the consent of all its partners in the Western European Union (WEU), the enlarged defence structure based on Bevin's original 1948 Brussels Treaty.

The fear of Germany, combined with the federalist momentum, had also inspired another French-led project, adjacent to the proposed EDC. With Spaak in the chair, a high-level Committee of the Six was negotiating another draft treaty, for a European Political Community (EPC). This was completed by February 1953. Article 1 again contained its essence: 'The present treaty sets up a European Community of a supranational character. The community is founded upon a union of people and states ... it shall be indissoluble'. But signature was delayed while further debate took place. With the collapse of the EDC in 1954, the EPC fell as well.

Looking back on this part of the story, one cannot help but be astonished at the strength of French concerns about Germany and by the vigour of the Euro-Federalists in pressing their solution. There was, after all, not just a NATO decision to rearm Germany but also to integrate German forces, along with those of other West European countries, in the American-led, command structure of NATO. There was no question of Germany being allowed to recreate its all-too-efficient German General Staff, let alone to be allowed to deploy for military purposes, other than self-defence, its own armed forces.

The question of Germany and the half century of peace that the European Continent has now enjoyed, still confuses debate in the UK about European issues generally. That most desirable period of peace has *not* been secured by the European Communities. German power has *not* been contained within the European treaty structures. Peace in Western Europe itself and between East and West during the Cold War have been secured above all by the North American military presence, its command and control structures. Certainly, the coming together of France and Germany is welcome and helpful, but it is simply myth-making to assert that it is this that has underpinned the half-century of peace on the Continent. NATO was and remains the great assurance and insurance of Continental peace in Europe. Long ago, in 1949, that blunt British soldier General Ismay, the first Secretary General of NATO, facing his first press conference and asked to sum up what the purposes of the new alliance were, responded thus: 'To keep the Russians out, to keep the Americans in and to keep the Germans down'. That is far nearer the truth than the myths of the Europhiles. But to it should be added that the restoration of political democracy and the rule of law in Western Germany, under the benign occupation of the US and the UK, made a massively important additional contribution.

So, with the collapse of the EDC and the EPC the federal thrust was brought to a halt. But not for long. With the indefatigable Jean Monnet and Paul Henri Spaak publicly spearheading the federal cause and with the active encouragement of the US State Department, what turned out to be the most successful integrationists initiative of all was launched at the 1955 Messina Conference, with Spaak – then Foreign Minister of Belgium – in the chair. The Conference produced a resolution authorising and guiding the further, prolonged negotiations that were concluded almost two years later in the Rome Treaties of 1957: the one establishing the European Economic Community or Common Market and the other, the Euratom Treaty, specifically concerned with the promotion of civil nuclear power by the Six. Spaak himself in his autobiography was with reason later to claim that they amounted to 'nothing short of a revolution'.

Given the previous failure of integration efforts in the areas of defence and political union, it was virtually inevitable that the new treaties should focus on the economic and industrial sectors, where integration measures would hopefully be more easy to agree but which would, by their own dynamism, lend themselves to further developments. But the Rome Treaty no less than the ECSC and the failed EDC and EPC treaties did not fail to restate the aim of 'ever closer union' and of creating a European Community, with the same essential structure of supranationalism and independent institutions that had distinguished the Monnet-Schuman original federal design. The specific economic features of the Rome Treaty were: the dismantling of all tariff and quantitative restrictions in trade between the Six nations; the erection of a common tariff wall around the Six against other countries; the free movement of labour, firms and capital between the Six; the establishment of an appointed, independent Commission in Brussels with sole powers of policy initiative and for policing the treaty agreements; a Council of Ministers to make, along with the Commission, policy decisions either by unanimous agreement or by qualified majority voting and an independent European Court of Justice, empowered to rule on disputes between member states and their citizens and corporations affected by Commission/Council decisions and legislation.

This indeed was a formidable and challenging development. Up to this point, it would be difficult to fault the design or execution of British post-war external policy, not only in relation to Europe but in the larger context of the Cold War and the successful, though still incomplete, transformation of Empire into Commonwealth. That of course has not prevented some Europhile writers of contemporary history from listing a long charge sheet of Britain's alleged sins of omission and commission in these years. Churchill, who did so much not only to sustain and ultimately liberate occupied Europe in war but also to inspire reconciliation and unity in peace, is a particular target for censure. According to Hugo Young, one of our contemporary journalist-historians, Churchill: 'Epitomised the characteristic consistently displayed by almost every politician ... who came after him: an absence of steady vision on the greatest question concerning the future of Britain in the last fifty years.' And again, 'Churchill was called the father of Europe ... but he was also the father of misunderstanding about Britain's part in Europe. He encouraged Europe to misunderstand Britain and Britain to misunderstand itself'. In fact, Churchill's approach to post-war Europe, far from leading to misunderstandings, was made patently clear from the beginning. He wanted the countries of Continental Europe to come much closer together in co-operation and union and, if they wished it, to the point of merging into a United States of Europe. Britain would be a friend and co-operator but Britain, with its Dominions and its Empire, would not and could not be part of that European close combination.

In the first of his great post-war orations, the Zurich speech of 1946, when Churchill was calling for the recreation of the 'European family' he was also stating that 'we British have our Commonwealth of Nations' and that while France and Germany must together take the lead in reuniting Europe 'Great Britain and the British Commonwealth, mighty America and I trust Soviet Russia must be the friends and sponsors of the new Europe'.

That really couldn't be clearer. In The Hague two years later, Churchill spoke of Britain joining a Council of Europe – which we did – and bringing with her the Empire and Commonwealth to create one of the world's pillars for stability and peace. At the Council of Europe meeting in August 1950, when Europe was still reeling from the brute fact and dangerous implications of the North Korean invasion of the South and the threat of Soviet armed power to Western Europe, Churchill did call for the immediate creation of a European Army 'in which we should all bear a worthy and honourable part'. The 'all' obviously included a UK contribution, if a European army were created.

True, Churchill did give the impression that a Conservative government would be more active in promoting European union than was the Attlee government. And Spaak for one did not abandon hope that Britain could be coaxed into the supranational quasi-federal structures of which the Schuman Plan was the founding model until 1952. In that year when the newly-elected Churchill government made absolutely plain that it was not going to join either the European Coal and Steel Community or the European Defence Community. But for Churchill's critics to blame, as they do, the British for the French abandonment of their own EDC project two years later is simply ludicrous. No one who has seriously studied Churchill's speeches in the earlier post-war years – in the House of Commons, at Party Conferences as well as on great occasions abroad – could have the slightest doubt as to where he stood.

Indeed a recent author of these complaints about Churchill contradicts himself when he makes his main charge against him that Churchill and his successors, Attlee and Eden, continued to conduct the nation's affairs as though we were still a world power. Among many scornful references, Hugo Young writes of the British belief that 'the Island Nation belonged not to the continent but to the world'. According to Mr Young and other critics, the British under their first three post-war prime ministers still had an inflated view of their own influence and power.

The target for particular attack is the framework thinking, the three concentric circles of interest and connection, to which Churchill frequently referred in describing both the constraints and the opportunities for Britain's influence and involvement. To quote Churchill's own words as spoken to the Conservative Annual Conference in Llandudno in 1948, 'the first circle for us is naturally the British Commonwealth and Empire, with all that comprises. Then there is also the English-speaking world in which we, Canada and the other British dominions play so important a part. And finally there is a United Europe'. It is clear, from the context and from numerous other speeches, that the United States was included in the second circle, the English-speaking world.

46

Churchill then went on to make the obvious and significant point: 'Now if you think of the three inter-linked circles you will see that we are the only country which has a great part in every one of them. We stand, in fact, at the very point of junction and here in this Island at the centre of the seaways and perhaps of the airways also we have the opportunity of joining them all together'. Just how much power and influence Britain then possessed and still possesses in those three circles is of course wide open to serious examination and debate. But the reality of their existence and the uniqueness of the UK, in being a part of all three, is simply not open to challenge.

Further, in the decade 1945-55 and for many years after, Britain was, if not a world power, a power with world-wide commitments – with hundreds of thousands of men still in arms, with large forces stationed not only in Germany but in the Middle East and South East Asia, and with a string of bases – Gibraltar, Malta, Cyprus, Aden, Singapore and Hong Kong – to be garrisoned and maintained. The economic burden on the UK was heavy. Defence expenditure as a proportion of GDP stood at 7.7 per cent in 1951-2 and never fell below 6 per cent until the mid-1960s. The gradual withdrawal of British power from these and other centres was of course proceeding but a peremptory pull-out, before conditions of stability could be achieved and successor governments installed, could well have led to violence and subversion. The Communist drive to take over Malaysia had to be withstood and defeated before Malaysian self-government could be established. Later, Indonesian forces had to be halted in Borneo before Britain could leave the area. The British presence was in the process of withdrawal from war-time-occupied Iraq, Iran, Libya, Palestine and from Egypt itself. Indeed, it was not until the late 1960s that the Wilson government took the decision to begin the process of withdrawal from 'East of Suez' – with the abandonment of the Singapore base, the evacuation of Abadan and the termination of the British protectorate in the Gulf States. Could all of this have been accelerated, brought forward by perhaps a decade? Possibly: but anyone who believed that the British presence could have been ended in the years before the 1957 Rome Treaty, simply hasn't read or understood the history of our time.

But the British record of creative and responsible decision-making in the post-war period was to be terribly marred by two gross errors of political judgement – made at almost the same time by the Eden government in the disastrous year 1956. First and most memorable was the ill-fated and ill-judged decision, in concert with France and Israel, to seize the Suez Canal and Base Area, following Nasser's own seizure of the canal in June 1956. The second was the foolish decision, in response to Spaak's invitation to Britain to join in the Messina and post-Messina discussions leading up to the Rome Treaty, to send not a Minister but a middle-ranking Board of Trade official simply to observe the proceedings. Mr Bretherton did his job and reported faithfully to his superiors in London. And yet, incredibly, as the discussions revealed the scope and implications of the emerging treaty, Ministers simply failed to respond.

I do not hold the view that, had a UK Minister attended the negotiations, a treaty that was significantly different and acceptable to the British would have emerged. Indeed if we had attended and if we had been able to veto what was basically unacceptable to us, then I have no doubt that the enterprise would have been aborted – only to be relaunched at some future date with the UK excluded, as in the ECSC Treaty.

But common sense alone should have made certain that a senior British Minister was there. And this sin of omission was only reinforced by the great aberration and folly, the sin of commission, when Britain and France invaded the Suez Canal – only to be forced into a humiliating capitulation under the combined threat of the USA and the USSR and worldwide condemnation in the UN and in the Commonwealth.

1. Post-War Europe

There was indeed to be a tremendous fall-out from these events: a fall-out whose significance was to be multiplied when the following year brought back to Paris and to presidential power the massive personal force of General de Gaulle.

But first to the immediate post-Suez effects. For France, the failure of the enterprise was at once to sour relations with her British partner. Whether, if the British government had defied international pressures, the French would have as well, one can only guess. But Britain, faced with a massive run on the pound and collapse of sterling, as well as exposure to all the threats and pressures of the Soviet Union and the United States, was the first to call a halt.

French resentment was also targeted at the United States, whose hostile intervention was seen to be the decisive factor in aborting the whole expedition. For the French, distrust of the Anglo-Saxons and the attraction of a developing partnership with the Six, where French influence was particularly strong, were part of the long-lasting legacy of the Suez affair.

For the United Kingdom, the psychological impact of the disaster was even greater. The humiliation was unforgettable and impossible to disguise. Two main lessons were learnt by the British political establishment. First – if anyone was so foolish even then to believe we retained it – we had lost the power against world opinion to embark upon major military expeditions, even with a partner as strong as France. And second, there was an imperative need to revive and sustain the Anglo-American alliance. But the loss of self-confidence was palpable and nowhere was it more strongly – and bitterly – felt than in the FCO and among the diplomats and politicians of the UK. The approaching completion of the Common Market Treaty negotiations – signed in Rome a few months after Suez in May 1957 – served to open British eyes as well to this new and potentially dangerous development in Europe that could adversely affect Britain's trade and economic prosperity.

The British response to this – though late in the day – was in fact very sensible: to create a Free Trade Area, throughout Western Europe, in which the Common Market would become a member. This would of course have allowed the Six to retain their supranational institutions; their commitment to 'ever closer union', the common policies which were then little more than gleams in the eye. But the trade preferences, sustained by its common external tariff, would not apply to the other European free trade partners – although it would still operate against non-European exporters.

Of course acceptance would have been very welcome to the British – and indeed to other non-EC European traders – and on merit, very difficult to fault. Negotiations were opened and vigorously pursued by the UK's able young trade Minister, Reginald Maudling, throughout 1957 and into 1958. Whether – but for the political earthquake of de Gaulle's return to power – it could have been accepted is impossible to assert with confidence but, on common sense grounds the mutual advantages to be gained were considerable.

But the arrival of de Gaulle in 1958 opened a decisive new chapter in the history of France, Britain and Europe. Among his first decisions was the abrupt withdrawal of France from the trade talks, and with that the termination of the free trade area negotiations. In his own memoirs, penned after his final retreat to Colombey-les-deux-Eglises in 1969, de Gaulle recalls a fascinating early meeting with Macmillan in June 1958 when, in the course of their exchanges, the British Prime Minister 'had suddenly declared with great feeling: 'The Common Market is the Continental System [Napoleon's counter blockade of Britain] all over again. Britain cannot accept it. I beg you to give it up. Otherwise, we shall be embarking on a war which will doubtless be economic at first but which runs the risk of gradually spreading into other fields'. De Gaulle was not impressed. His own assessment of the British Free Trade Area approach was that it had been made 'with the intention of undermining the project of

institutions that Spaak and his collaborators had so skilfully introduced in the Rome Treaty. Indeed he scorned it and put in its place his own unbending belief in a *'Europe de patries'*, a concert of independent nation states. He had no difficulty with the protectionism of the Common External Tariff and indeed was to insist, to the point of threatening to leave the organisation, upon the adoption of a Common Agriculture Policy that would wholly protect and reflect French agricultural interests.

What de Gaulle above all saw in the treaty framework of the Six was an opportunity to reinforce the pursuit of French national interests, with the additional weight of the partner nations. Ideally, the Common Market would become an echo chamber for the voice of France. With a friendly and compliant Germany (as the United Kingdom was soon to discover) France had good reason not to enlarge its then membership. There was of course the problem of the institutions themselves: the qualified majority voting provisions in the treaty and the independence, with its sole power of policy initiative, of the Brussels Commission. It was the conflict between the wishes of France and its normally docile partners in a matter of importance that led to the policy of the 'empty chair' which led on to the famous Luxembourg Compromise allowing de Gaulle to have his way – which was to play also some part in the deception and self deception of British politicians in the years that followed. At the expense of the United Kingdom, and in spite of the defeat of French efforts to keep Algeria as a *département* of metropolitan France and in spite of threatened army rebellions, by the early 1960s the power and influence of France, had substantially increased.

Paradoxically, the Gaullist block on the federalist threat within the Six, did not diminish the problems that were mounting for the UK in its relations with Europe. It simply replaced them with the whole weight of a resurgent France, determined to diminish British

and Anglo-Saxon power and influence wherever this could be
achieved.

2

The UK's Loss of Nerve in 1960 and after

By the end of the 1950s, the British public had largely forgotten the Suez disaster; the privations of nearly two decades of war and post-war austerity were at last coming to an end; Britain had 'never had it so good', so the election posters proclaimed – and Macmillan won the October 1959 General Election with a handsome, near 100 majority.

But if the electorate had suppressed its memories of Suez, the establishment had not. The implications were still sinking in and, with them, the searching questions as to the future role and position of the UK itself.

A mood of deep pessimism started to settle in the Foreign Office. One of the most vivid accounts of the new outlook is that given by a senior British diplomat, and later Euro-campaigner, Gladwyn Jebb, British Ambassador to France in the 1954-8 period who, like the whole Foreign Office had been excluded from the tightly held Anglo-French invasion plans. It was Suez, he later wrote, that 'started me off in a different train of thought'. As he put it, 'the old special relationship with America was no more; we had been unceremoniously deterred by our special ally from doing something we were determined to do. The humiliation was total.' How then should we proceed? 'My personal belief was that only by forming a greater Western Europe could we continue to wield any substantial influence on world events'.

His views are worth noting and quoting for two additional

reasons. First, he had been, like so many in the British establishment, an Atlanticist. In his memoirs he recalls a moment in 1948 when he himself was a possible candidate for the post of Secretary General to the new Council of Europe. He discussed this with his then Minister of State, Hector McNeil who 'became quite indignant and asked me whether I really thought that Europe was more important than the North Atlantic'. As he records: 'The idea of an Atlantic Community was the thing and that of joining Europe, was subsidiary. In 1948 this was a proposition which I did not really dispute and indeed there were few people in Whitehall who would have asserted the contrary.' Second, the loss of influence and power following the Suez debacle was particularly upsetting to him, as it was bound to be to the elite members of Britain's professional diplomatic corps who had assumed and enjoyed the UK's Great Power status – and were almost obsessively concerned lest we be excluded from 'the top table' of decision making.

A contemporary companion in gloom, later one of our most distinguished Ambassadors, Sir Nicholas Henderson, but then quite junior in the FOC – representing really another, younger and increasingly influential, generation – wrote a widely circulated valedictory despatch on his own retirement in 1979 and later, in 1987, a reflective autobiography, *Channels and Tunnels*, referred to above. For Henderson, however, it was not Suez so much as our allegedly missed opportunities after 1945 that were so damaging: 'We had every West European Government ready to eat out of our hands in the immediate aftermath of war ... we could have shaped Europe as we wished.' We didn't have either the 'spur of defeat' nor the 'strength which victory should have provided'. We were only 'marginally victorious in 1945'. We 'underestimated the recovery power' of our European neighbours, we were fatally misled by Churchill's 'three interlocking circles'. And so the lament proceeds with the author concluding, even when writing in 1987, that 'anybody who has responsibility for any aspect of our economic and industrial affairs is acutely aware of impending doom – unless we take drastic steps'.

And the remedy, if such there still be? Of course, he argues, we should have joined the Schuman Plan and the Common Market decades before we did but from now on there must be 'full and irrevocable commitment to Europe'. And the government must take on the 'task of explaining the Community to the British public rather than making it the scapegoat of all our ills'.

Sir Nicholas Henderson and Lord Gladwyn (as Gladwyn Jebb later became) were certainly not alone in their apprehension. Looking back on it all, and in the light of the numerous other personal accounts by contemporary high-ranking officials that have been published, something like a collective nervous breakdown, a loss of nerve, seems to have afflicted the British establishment. It was a mood of pessimism about the country's future which was to influence and, in turn, to be influenced by Britain's top political leaders, including crucially Prime Minister Macmillan.

A possible alternative explanation – or perhaps supporting analysis – that we simply lost our way was that offered by Anthony Nutting, Minister of State at the Foreign Office. He courageously opposed Suez at the time and was to lose soon thereafter not only his Ministerial post but his position as an MP as well. Interrogated, some years later, about the mood post-Suez he said: 'It just left us in a total vacuum, resenting everybody ... British foreign policy was left in a sort of void really, for several years, until we picked ourselves up and said well we have got to go in *some* direction'. Yes: but unhappily not the right one.

Nevertheless, the need to rethink and redefine Britain's external policy and role was clear. So too was the need to re-examine the UK's economic strategy and economic policies generally, in the light of the formation of the Common Market and the emergence of a substantial tariff wall around its boundaries. De Gaulle had wrecked the obvious alternative, the larger European Free Trade Area and while the UK had then gone ahead to form the smaller EFTA, the Europe of Seven, this seemed even then to be only a partial and temporary solution.

The initiative here came from within the civil service itself, in June 1960 following the appointment as Permanent Secretary to the Treasury of the energetic Sir Frank Lee. He involved – with Ministerial approval – virtually the whole Whitehall machine in the preparation of a question-and-answer document that squarely faced the alternatives that were emerging. The crucial conclusion reached was that the UK should now reverse its post-war policy and seek to join the Common Market as a full member. As the report correctly surmised: 'We cannot join the Common Market on the cheap. Joining means taking two far-reaching decisions. First we must accept that there will have to be a political content in our action – we must show ourselves prepared to join with the Six in their institutional arrangements and in any development towards closer political integration. Without this we cannot achieve our foreign policy aims (i.e. maximising our influence in world affairs). Second there must be a real intention to have a Common Market ... and in general we must accept the Common Tariff'. The report considered timing, and was against an immediate application preferring a delay of 12-18 months. It concluded, sensibly enough, that the sine qua non of the application was a successful preliminary sounding, above all with France. As the report put it, 'to launch another initiative (the other, presumably, being the European Free Trade Area) and receive a second rebuff would be disastrous'.

And so it was to be. Not one rebuff, but two, before at the third attempt, the British surrender of its own interests was sufficiently enlarged to be acceptable to the Six – and above all to France. Macmillan accepted this advice – except for the crucial last sentence – and shaped his policies accordingly. Among his first moves was to reshuffle the Cabinet to place known Euro-enthusiasts in the most sensitive posts: Christopher Soames to Agriculture, Duncan Sandys to the Commonwealth Office and, as co-ordinator and negotiator-in-chief, Edward Heath to be Lord Privy Seal and Foreign Office spokesman in the Commons. The formal application was to be made in Brussels by Heath on 10 October 1961.

Before then, as we have seen on other earlier occasions, the Cold War intruded on the affairs of Britain and the Six. Khrushchev had heightened tension in East-West relations by announcing in late 1958 that the Soviet Union would no longer accept the 1945 arrangements, temporary as they were then thought to be, for the four-power management of Berlin and for the four occupied zones of Germany. The menace of a further Berlin blockade was in the air and was to remain for more than two years before the Berlin wall was erected – and later still President Kennedy was to visit and to proclaim the continued commitment of the US in the four words: *'Ich bin ein Berliner'*. Meanwhile the Soviet Union was assembling a government for East Germany and giving it formal recognition as a sovereign state.

Two consequences were to flow from the new Soviet initiative. Adenauer, understandably, felt threatened and exposed to Soviet armed might and to the ambitions for reunification of the new Communist-dominated government in East Germany. Macmillan was anxious to avoid any precipitate action, seeking to defuse the tension and to press ahead with his long-harboured aim of arranging a new four-power Summit in Paris.

Adenauer felt rebuffed after a hasty visit to London and privately described Macmillan as another Chamberlain, an appeaser. Macmillan's own views of Adenauer are recorded with considerable and uncomplimentary frequency in his diaries. The two leaders disliked and distrusted each other. But there was more to it than that. As Con O'Neill, later to lead the British official negotiating team in

Brussels during the 1961-3 Macmillan-Heath application for entry, and a former Ambassador to Bonn was to record retrospectively: 'We didn't ever appreciate how 'un-British' in his outlook, how unappreciative of the British, how hostile to the British Adenauer really basically was from the start ... he didn't like England very much. He regarded us as some kind of maritime pirates, jolly good at swiping chunks of Africa and looking after our own interests, but not very reliable in a European context.' Not exactly a friend at court, when the UK did launch its first application. And of course it was precisely during this period that the de Gaulle-Adenauer positive chemistry was at its height, with de Gaulle resolutely and publicly standing by his new friend and ally and calling for no compromise with the Soviets over Germany.

Nor was Macmillan helped by the long-awaited Summit when at last it came in May 1960 – and was immediately aborted by the release of organised Soviet fury, aimed at the Americans, one of whose U2 spy planes was shot down over Soviet territory. Since Macmillan had been the chief sponsor of the Summit Conference, its failure and the contempt shown by Khrushchev for Britain, as well as America, certainly did not raise the personal prestige and self-confidence of Macmillan, or the influence of the United Kingdom.

Nor was this the only bad news for Macmillan and the UK in this post-election year. Ever since the Soviet Union had successfully launched its Sputnik in 1957, the offensive and defensive implications of nuclear weapons plus long-range rocket launchers – let alone space weapons – had had to be given prominence in British strategic thinking. The long-range nuclear-armed V-bombers were beginning to age and Britain's deterrent capability had to be refurbished. The project in which the government and Chiefs of Staff had heavily invested, the long-range rocket Blue Streak, had to be abandoned in 1960 on grounds of cost and inadequate effectiveness.

There was no UK replacement. Macmillan turned to his old friend

Ike, President Eisenhower, and was able to obtain for the UK an air-launch missile, Skybolt and the promise of a still not complete Polaris missile system some time in the future. In return the UK made available the lease of Holy Loch as a base for American nuclear submarines. A help certainly, but the UK dependence on continued American assistance in what was a crucial part of national defence was not a welcome development.

But it was on the economic front that things were going badly wrong. The 1959 election year boom could not be sustained. A serious gap opened up in the balance of payments in 1960, leading to a full-blown sterling crisis – to be followed by what was becoming a familiar retrenchment package of cuts in public investment, increases in taxation, the raising of interest rates and the general slowing down of industrial investment and consumer expenditure.

Indeed it was this, coming on top of a decade of disappointingly slow economic growth, and the simultaneous contrasting achievement of the economies of the Six in the 1950s, helped by Marshall Aid, the removal of tariffs and the surge in business confidence resulting in rapid and sustained expansion, that for many clinched the argument for Britain to join the European Common Market.

It is not too much to say that the wave of pessimism already described, now reinforced by a further wave of defeatism, swept the British establishment both on the economic and on the political and diplomatic fronts in these crucial years and were a dominant – almost certainly *the* dominant – influence on Britain's new European and world policies.

Some former diplomats have already been quoted. But many other very senior men have given their testimony to their feelings at the time and indeed for many years after. One of our most distinguished post-war Home Office civil servants, Eric (now Lord) Roll wrote thus in his significantly entitled *Where Did We Go Wrong*: 'One figure is worth quoting which is very much in line with the general thesis of relative economic decline. The average compound rate of growth of output between 1950 and 1973 was 2.5% in Britain ... with Japan at 8.4% at the head, followed by Germany at 5%, Italy at 4.8%, France at 4.2% and Canada at 3%'. The UK was falling far behind.

Even more gloomy, indeed openly capitulationist, was what a senior Board of Trade official, Sir Roy Denman had to say when reflecting on what was to become the Macmillan government's first attempt in 1961-3 to join the Common Market: 'Our aim was to secure acceptable terms of entry. In one sense the terms of entry were irrelevant. No sensible traveller on the sinking Titanic would have said: "I will only enter a lifeboat if it is well scrubbed, well painted and equipped with suitable supplies of food and drink".'

A particularly influential voice was that of former US Secretary of State, Dean Acheson. While in sartorial and other ways rather publicly Anglophile, Acheson had long had a critical, even hostile, view of Britain – most vividly demonstrated as early as February 1947 when, on being informed of the UK's reluctant decision to withdraw its protecting forces from Greece, he commented: 'The British are finished. They are through'. It was Acheson too who delivered that other bogusly philosophical and historical judgement on the UK in December 1962: 'Britain has lost an Empire and has yet to find a role' – a judgement lovingly and endlessly repeated by our own, self-hating Europhiles.

But, given his position as Permanent Secretary to the Foreign Office in 1956-60, those very crucial years, the stated views of Lord Inchyra, in an interview with the BBC interviewer Michael Charlton some years later, are particularly telling: 'The UK was in danger of being relegated to the second division. We never went in to get something out. We went in to prevent our being kicked down really to a lower league'. Quite simply, with the Prime Minister in the lead, the British establishment had lost its nerve.

The farce and failure of Britain's first abortive attempt to join the

Common Market has been told many times and needs here only a brief recall. Macmillan made his preliminary soundings in both Paris and Washington. In the latter, the news of the volte face in British European policy was greeted with enthusiasm – at least in the State Department where a departmental view had long been formed that membership would not just be good for Britain but for America too. Because once in, European external policy would largely reflect the UK's world interests and Atlantic perspective that the US rightly wished Europe to possess. In fact, a keen European, George Ball was at the State Department in charge of European affairs and was delighted when he learnt, first hand from his friend Sir Frank Lee, of Britain's new policy turn. Ball himself, coincidentally, was a close friend of Jean Monnet and had acted for Monnet as a professional lawyer during Monnet's war years in Washington. More important, Macmillan was to establish a genuine rapport with Ike's successor, the youthful President Kennedy who assumed office in the January of that crucial year 1961 – a rapport to be developed and sustained by the appointment to the British Embassy in Washington of David Ormsby Gore, an intimate of the Kennedy family.

Paris however was far from encouraging from the start. Certainly Macmillan did not secure, before opening formal negotiations, the successful 'preliminary soundings', the near assurance of French consent, which he and his colleagues had been so strongly urged to obtain – because a 'second rebuff would be disastrous'. Kennedy, visiting Paris in June en route for his confrontation with Khrushchev in Vienna a few days later, had been asked by Macmillan to press the UK's case for entry and to offer to share US nuclear know-how with de Gaulle. Kennedy did the first but not the second. It was not until November, some weeks after Heath's formal opening in Brussels that de Gaulle and Macmillan met together at Birch Grove. Macmillan obtained nothing then. But noted in his diary – one suspects accurately – that de Gaulle 'talks of Europe and means France'.

More important was their return meeting at the Château de Champs in June 1962. There was little encouragement there either – although a hint was dropped that Anglo-French nuclear collaboration would ease the entry process.

The Cold War once again intervened with the Cuban missile crisis – and was again to draw the US and the UK more closely together, to the chagrin of France. Before attending the Nassau Conference to which Kennedy had invited him, Macmillan insisted on one further prior visit to de Gaulle. Their talks were extensive, including the question of missile development, much in Macmillan's mind since news of the test failure of Blue Streak's replacement, Skybolt, had become public. It is possible that de Gaulle gained the impression that, if Skybolt's failure were confirmed, Macmillan would go for a joint Anglo-French replacement project. But Macmillan returned to London in deep gloom about de Gaulle and a second veto on British entry.

In Bermuda, after a command performance of brilliant persuasiveness, Macmillan picked up the pieces of Britain's independent nuclear deterrent and persuaded Kennedy to re-equip Britain's nuclear delivery system with the surest of all weapons, the Polaris missile. Yes: it would have to be permanently committed in patrolling and targeting to NATO's deterrent submarine force but, in a national crisis, it would revert to Britain's own command and control. Macmillan urgently pressed Kennedy to make a similar Polaris offer to de Gaulle. But Kennedy refused – and the evidence is that had he made the offer, it would have been rejected with scorn.

Macmillan's success with the 'cousins' – achieved against the strongest contrary urgings of George Ball and the State Department Europhiles – served only further to enrage the General. Three weeks later, on 14 January 1963, at one of his great press conferences in Paris, de Gaulle exploded his own political bombshell: the French veto on Britain's entry effort, a decisive *Non*.

2. The UK's Loss of Nerve in 1960 and after

The French President's main motivation was made crystal clear. Britain inside the Common Market would bring with her all those interests and considerations that she shared with the United States and her own Commonwealth in the other continents of the world. As de Gaulle put it in his own memorable words: 'England in effect is insular, she is maritime, she is linked through her exchanges, her markets, her supply lines, to the most diverse and often the most distant countries; she pursues essentially industrial and commercial activities, and only slightly agriculture ones. She has in all her doings very marked and very original habits and traditions. In short, the nature, the structure, the very situation that are England's differ profoundly from those of the Continentals.' In contrast, the Treaty of Rome was concluded between six close and neighbouring continental states: 'States which are, economically speaking, one may say, of the same nature. Indeed, whether it be a matter of their industrial or agriculture production, their external exchanges, their habits or commercial clientele, their living or working conditions, there is between them much more resemblance than difference. Moreover they are adjacent, they interpenetrate, they are an extension of each other through their communications ... They are joined in solidarity, first of all because of the consciousness they have of together constituting an important part of the sources of civilisation; and also as concerns their security, because they are continentals and have before them one and the same menace from one extremity to the other of their territorial entity'.

France wanted a European Europe. Britain, if allowed in, would enmesh the community in a wider Atlantic grouping. The time might come when Britain's own evolution might bring her closer and lead the country to 'moor itself alongside the continent'. But not yet. In immediate, practical terms, de Gaulle was giving further strong expression to his opposition to Atlantic hegemony, his continuing hostility to the United States and its Anglo-Saxon partner, the United

Kingdom. He was also making certain that, as the Common Market itself evolved its policies and institutions during its three-phase/twelve-year transition period, the strongest voice inside the Six would be that of France itself – assuming continued German acquiescence or support. And de Gaulle was also making clear the choice of partners that he had already less ringingly proclaimed when he first brought Adenauer to his house in Colombey: it was Germany not the United Kingdom which was to be his chosen partner.

As though to drive home this last point, only eight days after saying 'non' to UK entry, on 22 January 1963 Adenauer was to join de Gaulle in the Elysée for the formal signature of the Franco-German Treaty, with its provisions for quarterly meetings of Foreign and Defence Ministers and their Chiefs of Staff, for six-monthly meetings of Heads of Government, and with its declared purpose of consulting with each other on EC matters and on East/West relations before decisions were made. In the European Community, as further events were to demonstrate, France was creating a command institution, a decision-making policy centre that was to drive and direct EC policy for decades ahead.

So close were the two events – No to Britain, Yes to Germany – that Adenauer himself was somewhat embarrassed, protesting that when the treaty-signing arrangements in the Elysée had been made, he had no idea that the French were going to veto the UK's application a few days before. And quite a number of Germany politicians and leaders were unhappy about the meaning of the treaty, particularly in relation to the US and NATO, anxieties that were later to be expressed when the Bundestag attached a protocol to the Franco-German Treaty. But of course – and this is where the Adenauer/Macmillan mutual dislike may well have played a part – nothing was said or done by the other Five to form an effective protest.

For the United Kingdom, and its wretched Prime Minister, there was no comfort. Although there had been warning signs, it still came like a bolt from the blue. Macmillan was shattered; his government's main political and economic policy plank had been destroyed. As he was to confide to his diary at that time, 'all our policies at home and abroad are in ruins'.

The years 1960-1, with the collapse of the Paris Summit, had been bad enough. 1961-2 with British nuclear policy virtually in ruins and the economy again in crisis was just as bad. But 1962-3, with the total collapse of his effort to join the Common Market, justly deserves the title of Macmillan's 'annus horibilis'.

Years later, when interviewed by the BBC on the publication of the second volume of his memoirs, Macmillan's bitterness still came through in his attempt to explain de Gaulle's conduct: 'He had a real hatred of the Americans and a kind of love/hate complex about the British. The truth is – I may be cynical but I fear it is true – if Hitler had danced in the streets of London, we'd have had no trouble with de Gaulle. If we had given in to Hitler we'd have had no trouble with de Gaulle. What they couldn't forgive us is that we held on and that we saved France. People can forgive an injury but they can hardly ever forgive a benefit'.

Perhaps. But in saying No to the United Kingdom, de Gaulle was speaking the essential truth about Britain: an Island, yes, but maritime, global in its interests and its reach as well. And it was Macmillan who had given in, thanks to his own pessimism and sense of failure, not to Hitler, but to the urgings and demands of a defeatist establishment who persuaded him to sue for entry to the Common Market on terms that were little more than a capitulation.

Interestingly, in a little-noticed further exchange at the same historic press conference in Paris, de Gaulle was to say that nothing would prevent an agreement for an 'association' of the UK with the EC 'designed to safeguard exchanges' and the further co-operation of France with the UK in high technology projects of which the Concorde aircraft was then the prime recent example.

But the UK establishment, and particularly the Foreign Office, now increasingly dominated by a new regiment of Europhiles, had burnt its boats. For them, there could be now no going back. And so, tragically, the scene was set for further humiliations and disasters.

Macmillan's bid for Common Market membership had not gained much favour in the UK. A significant number of Conservative MPs were opposed to entry and the official Opposition, the Labour Party, while welcoming the coming together of the Six, was strongly opposed to the terms of entry already agreed by Heath in his negotiations in Brussels (published as a White Paper in July 1962). In particular, Labour's then leader, Hugh Gaitskell, rightly saw that the customs union and Community preference policies of the treaty would not only discriminate against Commonwealth trade but would inevitably weaken and threaten the whole Commonwealth connection. Still more fundamentally, he recognised and opposed the supranational content of the Treaties and their clear implication for the UK's continued self-government and democracy. He was not prepared, as he so eloquently stated, to bring to an end 'a thousand years of British history'.

Illness and death were to remove Gaitskell from the political scene almost at the moment of de Gaulle's exercise of the French veto in January 1963. His successor, Harold Wilson, certainly then held views on the Common Market almost identical with those of his predecessor.

It is this that makes so puzzling Wilson's own conduct of European policy in government, after the election victories of 1964 and 1966. In particular what prompted him to make Britain's second application to join the EC in 1967? Up to the 1966 General Election, I had myself been very close to Wilson, in the Opposition years as Head of the Labour Party's Research Department and from 1964, when I was myself elected to Parliament, as the PM's Parliamentary Private Secretary. In the 1966 election campaign, with Heath then Leader of the Conservative Opposition, the Common Market was inevitably an election issue. It was then, on 18 March 1966 at Bristol, in what was at the time considered to be a defining speech, that Wilson denounced those unacceptable features of the Common Market in the most scathing terms. Of course, he made the usual genuflection: 'We shall go in if the terms are right'. But this was more than counter-balanced with 'Nothing could be worse if vital British and Commonwealth interests are to be safeguarded than to enter these negotiations, as we did before, cap in hand (promising in advance) to accept whatever conditions are offered to us'. As that powerful and rigorously intellectual anti-marketeer Douglas Jay has recorded: 'I was frankly overjoyed when I read these words'. I can myself vouch for Jay's optimistic interpretation because, unusually – for Wilson was always his own principal speech-writer – I had myself been involved in both discussing and drafting that Bristol speech, which was clearly rejectionist in both language and intent. This stance was however soon to change, with the Labour government making its own entry application in the spring of 1967.

At the time, and in the events that preceded it – the Chequers meeting of the Cabinet and the agreement that Harold Wilson and George Brown should jointly undertake a reconnaissance of the capi-tals of the Six before making any decision about a further British application – my interpretation was that, reacting both to pressures for a pro-European policy from within his own Labour party and still more from the Heath-led Opposition, Wilson was determined to put the issue to rest by demonstrating, from direct talks with the Leaders of the Six, that nothing of substance had changed since 1963 and that British membership just wasn't on.

I have thought much about this since and I can only conclude that I was hopelessly wrong – if not wholly about the original motive for the reconnaissance, then at least about the result. For, when de Gaulle had pronounced the second French veto in November 1967, even before formal negotiations had commenced, instead of abandoning the whole approach, and telling his critics 'I told you so', Wilson came out with the stupefying statement that: 'We won't take No for an answer'.

This and subsequent events, including the advanced preparations made to apply yet again in the summer of 1970 and Wilson's support for the 'Yes' vote in the 1975 Referendum, made clear that he had radically shifted his position. I have talked to those who, apart from myself, had frequent access to Wilson during this period and my conclusions are these: Wilson, like Macmillan before him, became increasingly pessimistic about the prospects before the UK. Like Gaitskell, he had a genuine concern and feeling for the Commonwealth but found in his dealings with them in the mid-Sixties and after increasing tension and estrangement. With apartheid rampant in South Africa and white supremacy entrenched in Salisbury (then Rhodesia), the Commonwealth was both increasingly demanding of, and critical of, the United Kingdom, and its agenda was dominated by the issue of anti-racism, both within the Commonwealth and in the United Nations, to the exclusion of virtually all other matters. Meetings with Commonwealth Heads of Government were increasingly fraught and unhappy events.

With the United States, while Wilson shared more than a little domestic policy overlap with President Johnson, particularly in the latter's 'great society' concept and while he successfully and crucially resisted intense American pressure for UK military support in Vietnam, Vietnam itself was a running sore in the Anglo-American relationship, with Wilson against his own convictions, giving minimalist verbal endorsement to the American cause.

But the decisive factor was the economy. Wilson had inherited a severe balance of payments crisis in October 1964 and the emergency measures that he had felt obliged to take, in particular the tax on imports, the import surcharge, had by 1966 proved to be only temporarily effective and at the same time deeply destructive of the relationships between the UK and her partners in EFTA whose exports to Britain could not be exempted. Worse was to come. The summer of 1966 produced a further balance of payments and sterling crisis, with the necessary countermeasures involving once again a halt to economic growth in the British economy. And even that was far from the end of an increasingly dismal story. November 1967 brought the long delayed devaluation of the pound, a further package of expenditure cuts and increased taxation, measures that had again to be intensified in late 1968-9. At home, Wilson failed to carry Cabinet, the Parliamentary Labour Party and the Trade Unions in implementing his income and anti-strike policies.

In the face of such events, the natural buoyancy of Wilson's temperament, together with the optimism that lay behind his original 'forging a New Britain in the white-hot heat of the technological revolution' were both to founder.

Of course, there were excellent and serious counterweights to the Europhiles in both the civil service and Foreign Office, particularly from the Treasury with Sir William Armstrong at its head, the Ministry of Agriculture with Sir John Winnifrith and the penetrating, though frequently derided, contributions made by the then Economic Advisers, including Lords Balogh and Kaldor.

The weight of establishment opinion however was heavily and persistently in favour of UK entry. The placing of the very able and ardent Europhile, Michael Palliser, (later Permanent Secretary at the FCO) in the key post of joint Private Secretary to the Prime Minister at No 10, with instant and daily access to the PM, at the minimum made certain that no Euro-sceptic critique or argument went unchallenged. Among other personal factors, the continued advocacy of Roy Jenkins from his very influential posts in the Cabinet, first as Home Secretary and then, after devaluation, as Chancellor and the ready access to the Prime Minister of Cecil King, the proprietor of Labour's one normally reliable mass-circulation newspaper, the *Daily Mirror*, must be counted.

But it was events, not people, that were the decisive factors. And so Wilson himself became a supporter of UK membership – reluctantly and without enthusiasm at any stage, the epitome and embodiment of the British attitude to the Common Market in the decades that followed.

The 1970 General Election returned the Conservatives to government, this time under the leadership of Edward Heath. The new negotiations began within weeks of the new government taking office. As Geoffrey Rippon, Heath's main negotiator, was frequently to allege, they simply 'picked up the hand' that had already been prepared by their predecessors, and played it.

As I was years later to discover, having consulted the Cabinet papers during the period when I was a Member, a subcommittee of Labour's leading Europhiles had been set up in 1969 with the task of preparing positions and papers for a renewed British application. Cabinet as a whole, myself included, was not aware of this work and of course it is true that the subcommittee report would, had Labour won in 1970, have had to be approved by full Cabinet before the application could proceed.

The fact of its existence did not of course make it easy for Labour, again in Opposition, to carry conviction in opposing and criticising the new Heath initiative. Fortunately for myself, when I became Labour's spokesman on Europe in October 1971, I was still totally unaware of the subcommittee's work and was able therefore without embarrassment to attack Rippon, in his monthly report-back from Brussels; to lead in the famous October debate on the White Paper outlining the agreed terms; to take apart the Treaty of Accession when published in January 1972 and then to mount a sustained assault during the whole prolonged debate, on the floor of the House, on the European Community's Bill that brought the treaty into affect from 1 January 1973.

Looking back on all this, I can certainly understand why those in the former Labour Cabinet who held a strong opposing view on the European Community should feel rather disappointed by the Party's policy shift so soon after we entered Opposition, particularly if those on the European subcommittee had, wrongly, assumed that their preparations and activities were known to all their colleagues.

But to return to the Heath-Rippon application: if one negotiating party is determined to surrender, it doesn't normally take long to agree the terms. There was of course the problem of a wary, even hostile British public opinion that Heath had to watch, and Parliament too, with the Labour Party once more swinging into serious opposition and with disquiet among many of his own backbenchers. But these were obstacles that Heath was easily able to overcome, particularly after receiving the decisive voting support of the sixty nine Labour Jenkinsites, rebels, Labour's Europhile MPs, who ensured a continued parliamentary majority for Heath. They even supported him when the government guillotined the debate, and even when the constitutional outrage that the treaty inflicted upon the supremacy of Parliament and the ultimate authority of the British Courts was clearly exposed. And so, to enter the Common Market, Britain basically abandoned its long-developed low-cost food supplies from Canada, Australia and New Zealand and became a second stomach for the high cost surpluses of French farmers. Imperial preference – tariff-free access to the UK market of Commonwealth manufactured goods – already much reduced in its effects, was not just abandoned but Commonwealth manufacturers were now also subjected to the impositions of the Common Market's external tariff.

The institutional structure, the Commission and the European Court of Justice, their voting system in the Council of Ministers, along with the volumes of European legislation – the Directives and regulations enacted since 1958 – all were accepted without amendment, apart from a token butter quota allowed for New Zealand and a sugar quota for the Island cane producers of the Commonwealth.

At first sight, the terms negotiated by Geoffrey Rippon were not much different from those that Macmillan had been presented with in 1961-3, before the first French veto. But on closer examination two significant additional items emerged. First the requirement on all member states, including the applicant UK (and Eire, Denmark and Norway), to introduce a new system of indirect taxation, value added tax, VAT. The pre-entry UK system of high purchase tax on what was then regarded as luxury and semi-luxury items, with total purchase tax exemption on necessities such as food, and clothing, had to be replaced, and without delay, by the new VAT tax system. Second, and much more important, the UK had to accept the Community's new system of self-taxation – to raise the monies needed to finance the range of common policies, of which the French-designed Common Agriculture Policy was far and away the most expensive – the so-called 'own resources'.

The French and the other Common Market countries knew of course of the British government's intention of making a further application – which they judged, correctly, would follow fairly promptly after de Gaulle himself had finally retired in April 1969. And they prepared for the event. The twelve year transition period which began on 1 January 1958 was due to end on 1 January 1970. Up to that date, the Community had financed itself in what any outsider would consider to be a reasonably fair and acceptable way: each country contributed the same percentage of its GDP. So, the larger and richer states paid more while the smaller and poorer states paid less. Should this continue at the end of the transitional period or should an alternative system be adopted – one that would take account not only of the completion of the Common Market but its expected enlargement as well?

2. The UK's Loss of Nerve in 1960 and after

Two years before his retirement, de Gaulle had not for nothing placed his then Prime Minister, Pompidou, in 'the reserve of the Republic'. Pompidou then took over the reins of the Presidency from de Gaulle as President of France. On a French proposal, a special conference of Heads of Government was held at the Hague in December 1969 and agreement reached on a range of matters including the opening of negotiations for enlargement and the new taxes that were to replace the former percentage GDP contributions. The new taxes were these: the yield of all the customs duties imposed on goods imported from outside the Six; a new system of agriculture levies, a variable tax, imposed upon imports of foreign-produced food so that food imports could never undercut the farm prices guaranteed for the Community's own-produced food; and third, a percentage of the yield of the new compulsory VAT.

Nobody who studied the impact of this new tax system, in particular, the differential yield from customs duties and levies on imported food, could have any doubt as to which country would be obliged to pay a contribution far in excess of what the previous system would have demanded – the UK. For Britain it was like a tax on British history, a tax on the Commonwealth itself, a huge gross impost, negligibly offset by the revenue flow of agricultural support funds because the UK's agriculture industry itself was, proportionately, the smallest in Europe.

The estimated burden, the net payment added to the UK's chronic balance of payments problem was too vast even for a demanding France and a feeble Heath to accept as an obligation from Day One of membership. Instead the United Kingdom was allowed a special seven-year transition period in which it would pay a gradually increasing percentage of its agreed sum until, at the end of the seven years, the full burden would be imposed.

One further last-minute policy initiative was put in place, immediately before the Heath negotiating team arrived in Brussels.

Appearing as from nowhere, just days before Britain's formal application ceremony in Brussels, was the hastily constructed Common Fisheries Policy which, while permitting the UK its continued near-exclusive use of its own coastal waters, within the traditional six to twelve mile limit, claimed for the Community the newly-agreed two-hundred mile limit that the United Nations Conference on the Sea had allowed coastal and island states. It thus brought the great fishing areas of the North Sea, the Irish Sea, the South West approaches and the North Atlantic – formerly dominated by UK trawlers – into Community ownership and control, in which the UK was henceforth to be allowed only a quota.

The negotiations were virtually completed by the summer of 1971. This time, long before the White Paper had been written and voted on in the crucial October debate in Parliament, Heath had made his personal peace with France. Returning from his visit to Pompidou in May 1971, Heath was able to report to the House that he had been heartened to 'discover how close are the views of the French and British governments on the development of Europe and its role in the world. Our talks showed that both governments wished to bring about the development of a unified Europe through an enlarged European Community'.

Not only was Britain happy with the Community as it was, but 'Britain looked forward wholeheartedly to joining in the economic and monetary development of the Community ... the President emphasised the importance he attached to the system of Community preference and his welcome for Britain's acceptance of this principle immediately upon entry to the Community'.

On the heavily disadvantageous financing arrangements, Heath, pressed by Wilson, had said that it had been discussed with Pompidou and that he, Heath, told the French President that 'I thought these would help to remove any suggestion that we were not accepting the full system of Community financing'.

76

2. The UK's Loss of Nerve in 1960 and after

Altruism or capitulation could hardly go further, though Heath did add that there was agreement that the 'actual arrangements, to be satisfactory, must not place an unbearable burden on the balance of payments'. Among the many considerations which shaped Heath's whole approach was, in his own words, his belief that the European Community was 'the best means, and probably the only means in the world today of guaranteeing peace within Europe, providing prosperity for her peoples and restoring to Europe that political, economic and cultural influence in the world that her traditions and her potential justify'; and further that the European Community will 'by its unity be of a size and nature in equal position with the United States, Japan or the Soviet Union' in world trade and financial affairs.

So, driven by his own enthusiasm and growing sense of mission and backed by Europhiles in all the political parties, in the establishment, in business and elsewhere, negotiations were concluded, the treaty signed, the bill debated, resisted and enacted. For the UK the die was cast and basically the settlement obtained at the end of 1971 was to endure for the following eight years.

Of course an attempt was made to break the shackles of the treaty when Labour was returned again to office in 1974, with a Manifesto commitment to undertake a 'fundamental renegotiation' of the terms of entry. In practice, it turned out to be a mainly cosmetic exercise: when the results were put to the electorate in the promised referendum, the decision to stay in was taken by a two-to-one majority in the poll.

After that, with a much more limited objective, but one which was pursued with tigerish persistence and energy, Mrs Thatcher, elected Prime Minister in 1979, fought and won her four-year battle to reduce by one-half the punitive and unacceptable burden placed on Britain by the 'own-resource' tax system. Even so, in the period since the UK joined in 1973, our net payment (our contribution after allowing for receipts) amounted to the staggering total of £40 billion and is now running at roughly £2-3 billion a year.

In Brussels itself and in the Community generally the quarter century was a period of at best consolidation at worst, euro-sclerosis. Ironically for the UK, the EC, faced like Britain at the very moment of entry with the enormous shock and on-going burden of OPEC's quadrupling of oil prices, was obliged to reduce its formerly rapid economic growth to a crawl. With a further doubling of oil prices in 1979, it became clear that the days were over when the European Community could be regarded as an area of high and sustained economic growth. Unemployment increased and competitiveness declined as new social policies joined higher energy costs to raise the price of Community exports.

Perhaps with good reason, no government has attempted to assess the UK's overall costs and benefit since its membership in 1973. It would not be easy to do so, not least because of the initial heavy and adverse impact of the oil shock, then the remarkable development of Britain's own oil and gas supplies from the North Sea and, on top of these, the adoption of the emerging fashionable doctrines of monetarism, from the Chicago school, in the conduct of the UK's economic policies. Finally, any attempt at an assessment would have to take account of the two most significant developments of all in the 1970s and 80s: the abandonment of fixed currency exchange rates and the end of the dominance of trades union organised labour in determining the costs, the prices and the competitiveness of British industry.

But one thing is certain. The twenty five years that followed the UK's entry into the Common Market were anything but a period of enhanced prosperity for the United Kingdom. GDP grew, but only slowly, even more slowly than in the rest of the EC; unemployment rose not once, but twice to record, above 3 million, post-war levels and great swathes of British industry were wiped out. Whatever else it achieved, the EC did not bring prosperity to Britain. There were attempts to restore some momentum to European affairs, but after the Jenkins Presidency in 1979 had created the European Monetary System (EMS), with its operating arm the Exchange Rate Mechanism (ERM), and the ecu, its European currency, the integration project ground to a virtual stop.

One institutional initiative did come, not surprisingly, from Jean Monnet and his Action Campaign for a United States of Europe when, once again exploiting his incomparable network of personal contacts, he floated his scheme for a European Provisional Government following direct approaches to Willy Brandt, then Chancellor of the German Federal Republic, Michel Jobert in Pompidou's Cabinet and Edward Heath, then still Prime Minister. He did achieve in the following year 1974 the agreement of their successors – Giscard d'Estaing, Schmidt and Wilson – to the formation of a new supreme European Council, the Council of Heads of Government, to meet henceforth at regular twice-yearly intervals to provide a continuing direction, from the very top, of European affairs. It is interesting to note that when presented with Monnet's initial proposals, Heath's response was, 'I'll accept that but not the title Provisional Government. That would get me into great difficulties. "Supreme Council" would be closer to the facts. On the other hand, a meeting every three months would not be enough. Why not every month?'

At the December 1974 meeting, at the end of the French Presidency, Giscard d'Estaing ended the meeting with these words, 'The Summit is dead: long live the European Council'. Thus was a further and important piece of architecture added to the structure of the European Community.

The only other initiative certainly worthy of mention in this twenty-five-year period came, oddly enough, from the British in the person of Mrs Thatcher, then Prime Minister. No one could say that

Mrs Thatcher had lost her nerve, either about the country which she was repeatedly elected to govern or about the correctness of her own views and policies on the subject of capitalist and competition policies. Encouraged no doubt by her success over the British rebate, and having placed a former trusted and competent Minister, Cockfield in Brussels as one of the UK's two commissioners, Mrs Thatcher launched her policy initiative in 1985 with proposals to radically extend the existing Common Market into a Single Market. This involved the dismantling of non-tariff trade barriers, the extension of competition into services and utilities and the championing of privatisation of state industry and of de-regulation everywhere.

In extending market forces and creating a Single Market, Mrs Thatcher found that provisions for unanimity in various parts of the Treaties an impediment to agreement: her solution was for the Community to adopt a 'convention' – curiously similar to, though in effect precisely the opposite of, de Gaulle's Luxembourg Accord – in which, in making decisions, unanimity would be replaced by qualified majority voting, except in those cases where 'vital national interests' were involved. At the Milan Heads of Government Council meeting that summer, the integrationists turned the tables on the British Prime Minister. They agreed, not only to the general thrust of her Single Market proposals but to establish an Inter-Governmental Conference to devise and agree those treaty amendments that would give them effect. Mrs Thatcher, who did not want any extension of formal treaty powers, was furious but helpless: the IGC was established, itself by qualified majority vote in the Council and the treaty amendments which later emerged could hardly be vetoed by their principal author.

Worse was to come. The new Single European Act Treaty, lovingly nurtured by the recently appointed President of the Commission Jacques Delors, contained the usual lengthy preamble about the integrationists aims of the Community including its long-affirmed purpose of creating an Economic and Monetary Union. Moreover the treaty provisions established no clear frontier between the area of economic decision making and the adjacent and overlapping areas of social policy. Mrs Thatcher signed it – and the process of ratification was then set in train.

As Mrs Thatcher was soon to discover, preambles and declarations in European Treaties are not just rhetoric and guff but confer legitimacy on further initiatives to implement them. The PM's failure to recognise that what she had agreed to was not just an extension of free-market practices in the European Community but a major change in the decision-making process there and a matter of great constitutional importance, was reflected in its treatment in the House of Commons. Virtually no time was allowed for the committee stage of the enabling Bill, before a guillotine brought any worthwhile examination to a halt. The Labour Front Bench, reflecting the new passivity and me-tooism on European issues of the middle and later period of Kinnock's leadership, was both deliberately passive and largely unaware of the provisions in the bill. The Treaty and the Single European Act were thus allowed to become law with hardly a serious comment in the media or any substantial examination in Parliament to mark its passage.

Mrs Thatcher's chagrin at the outcome of her Single Market initiative was undoubtedly genuine – as was the glee of a number of her European Community colleagues who did little to conceal their satisfaction at the success of this ambush. No Minister, let alone one as energetic and demanding with herself as well as with others as Mrs Thatcher, can escape responsibility for their own decisions. But no one who has been engaged seriously in the business of examining draft EC laws and treaties can have any doubt about their quite extraordinary – and deliberate – complexity. Every new article or treaty clause is, with reference to articles in earlier treaties – generally to be located in a separate treaty volume. Indeed part of the whole mystique of Community Law is its textual incomprehensibility, its physical dispersal, its ambivalence and its dependence upon ultimate clarification by the European Court of Justice: and the Brussels Commission and their long-serving, often expert officials are, in interpreting and manipulating all this, like a priestly caste – similar to what it must have been in pre-Reformation days, when the Bible was in Latin, not English; the Pope, his cardinals and bishops decided the content of canon law and the message came down to the laymen, only when the Latin text was translated into the vernacular by the dutiful parish priest. Yes, very, very difficult. But the texts can be penetrated and understood and, if combing through the minutiae is hardly to be expected of a twenty-hour-a-day Prime Minister, surely the army of trained officials in the FCO could be relied upon to do the detective work and to flash the warning lights.

Did they? I do not know but I strongly suspect that Mrs Thatcher's growing exasperation with the FCO and its Europhile Secretary of State, Geoffrey Howe, and her increasing dislike of Delors personally, the Commission as an institution and the supranational ambitions of her Council colleagues had, with the passage of the Single European Act (SEA), already turned her into a Eurosceptic even before the great new integrationist thrusts of the late 1980s were to be unleashed.

3

The Berlin Wall, Maastricht

Still Closer Union

On 10 November 1989, Soviet troops simply watched as the Civil Authorities and ordinary citizens of East Berlin tore down the Berlin Wall. It was the beginning of the end of the two Germanies. Erected by the Soviets in October 1961, the Wall had done much to drive France and a frightened West Germany still closer together, culminating in the Franco-German Treaty of January 1963. Now once more, it was to play a decisive role in European affairs and in the policies of both France and Germany.

Three months after its demolition, in February 1990, Chancellor Kohl was in Moscow, urging and obtaining Gorbachev's consent to the reunification of East with West Germany and by July, Gorbachev had accepted that the reunified Germany should remain in NATO.

The collapse of the Berlin Wall signalled the general collapse of Eastern Europe's Communist regimes and, barely two years later, of Communism in the Soviet Union and the disintegration of the USSR itself into the eighteen separate nation states that now form the so-called Commonwealth of Independent States.

The collapse of the Berlin Wall marked a moment of massive change, another turning point in post-war history. Nowhere were the consequences felt more intensely than in Germany itself and in its partner France – and in the European Community in which France and Germany exercised so powerful, indeed dominating, an influence.

For France the whole post-war scene had, almost overnight, changed. The Federal German Republic, France's neighbour since the late 1940s, was numerically no larger in population than France itself. Its original status as the three Western zones of a defeated and occupied state, ensured for France an initial and continuing seniority in their partnership – beginning with the 1950 Schuman Plan and reinforced as it was by the dominating personality and presence of de Gaulle in the whole decade before his retirement in 1969. Since then, something approaching equality had been gained as West Germany's economic and industrial power continued to grow at a faster pace than that of her Western neighbour. But now, with a reunited Germany, a Germany of 80 million people, the old partnership was bound to change. For France, to retain equality would be an achievement; to be forced into the junior partner role the more likely development.

For France, with its overriding and abiding concern to contain, permanently, German power the great question had again to be answered: how, in these new circumstances, was the safety and security of France to be best achieved?

For several years before these dramatic and traumatic events, French policy makers had been concerned with the continuing growth of German economic power and in particular at the dominance of the DMark over the French Franc and other European currencies. The German achievement of price stability at home and the strength abroad of the DMark gave Western Germany a dominant position in the Exchange Rate Mechanism – forcing the partner nations, including France, to periodically alter (generally to devalue) their exchange rates to be competitive with their dominant neighbour and forcing them to change their interest rates in line with the Bundesbank's decisions in Bonn.

For the French, particularly for Giscard d'Estaing and his successor François Mitterand, the continued dominance of the Bundesbank and the DMark had led to the conclusion that it would be in the interest of France and help bring about an increase in her influence in the setting of exchange rate and interest rate policies, if they were to bring the DMark under European control, through the creation of a single currency. The development of an Economic and Monetary Union (EMU) had of course featured much earlier in the ambitions of the Euro integrationists. The Werner Report in the 1960s had recommended such a currency merger and, in the 1972 Summit meeting, while not specifically mentioned, EMU was indeed part of that transformation of 'the whole complex of their relations into a European Union by the end of a decade' that Heath had so enthusiastically endorsed at the time.

Moreover the positioning of people and power was exceptionally favourable to a renewed integration move. The Commission President, re-appointed in 1989 for a further term, was the able and experienced former French Finance Minister, Jacques Delors, who was particularly close to Mitterand and who also established a very close relationships with Chancellor Kohl. Mitterand and Kohl enjoyed excellent personal relationships – even unhealthily close, if recent allegations of illicit French financing of the CDU turn out to be true. But, standing together, side-by-side, hand in hand on many commemorative occasions, they were indeed symbols of that reconciliation between the two old enemies for which Adenauer and de Gaulle had laid the foundations and which Churchill for one, with his call for 'Teuton and Gaul' to end their historic enmity forty years earlier, had so urgently pressed. Kohl, re-elected as Chancellor, dominated the German and increasingly the European political scene, last of that line of German leaders to have personally experienced, and felt the guilt and shame of, Nazi rule. So the two power centres of the European Community, the Franco-German Treaty partnership and the Brussels Commission with its European Treaty prerogative of policy initiation, were at one in the new single currency drive – even before the Berlin Wall, so unexpectedly, came down.

Indeed it was Kohl himself who proposed at the Hanover Council in June 1988 that a Committee of Central Bank Heads should be set up, to report back in 1989 on the achievement of an Economic and Monetary Union – a Committee of which Delors himself, at Kohl's suggestion, was to be the Chairman.

The Committee duly reported in April 1989 in favour of the EMU project, with a European Central Bank and a single European currency at the end of a three-phased transitional period. With Mrs Thatcher objecting, a majority decision established yet another IGC to carry forward the EMU project and to prepare the necessary treaty amendments. Kohl's dominance in Germany politics was never more obvious and necessary, for the project had to surmount the open opposition of the Bundesbank's President and much of German public opinion for whom the Bank and the DMark were proud symbols of national revival and success.

This then was the immediate European Community background to the historic events of the demolition of the Berlin Wall, Germany re-unification and the collapse of East European Communism. For France, the very welcome success in the currency and monetary fields, had now to be set against the new reality of German unity and enhanced German power.

There is no doubt of French unease, nor that it was fully shared by Mitterand himself. Mitterand and Thatcher talked frankly about it. The choices for France were basically only two. One was to find ways of delaying the formal reunification of Germany's two halves, while reshaping the German alliance and by bringing in the British to form a triumvirate – with France and the UK together outweighing the reunited Germany. The other, drawing the noose of Community law and policy still more tightly around Germany, by extending the supranational competence of the European Treaties into even wider policy areas. Mitterand chose the latter course and consequently Gaullism was largely banished from the Elysée.

3. *The Berlin Wall, Maastricht*

To give effect to the new integrationist drive a second IGC was almost simultaneously launched, with the remit of advancing the political competence of the Community, of forming a European Union. The aim was no less than to bring together the foreign and security policies and as soon as possible, the defence policies of the member states as well, in a common treaty framework. Even French anxieties, German compliance and Brussels enthusiasm together could not easily storm these last bastions of the independent state in a single assault. But significant progress was made.

After the two IGCs completed their work in late 1990, the basic shape of what was, a year or so later, to become the Maastricht Treaty began to emerge: detailed proposals for a European common security and foreign policy; acceptance, in principle that this could later embrace a common defence policy; still more progress, practical as well as symbolic, in creating One Europe, an area with external but no internal frontiers; the development of a common policy for immigration and asylum; the three-phase plan for an EMU, with its detailed rules for the macro-economic conduct and supervision of member states and with the aim within a decade of establishing a single currency and a European Central Bank – an integrationist leap towards the final goal of a European state that none but the blind could fail to recognise. As the new treaty's introductory preamble rightly but modestly claims: 'This Treaty marks a new stage in the process of creating an ever-closer union among the peoples of Europe'.

If the French had found what they hoped would be a solution to the new German problem and if the Federalists rejoiced at their biggest success yet in advancing towards a European State and in the progressive demolition of the Nation State, no similar rejoicing was to be heard in London.

Mrs Thatcher, of course, well before the fall of the Berlin Wall and the boost to European integration that it gave rise to, had made clear her own dissatisfaction with the European Communities' institutions and policies, her resentment at the exploitation of her own initiative on the Single Market and above all her belief, not in an increasingly supranational Europe but in a looser association of independent nation states which should be joined, as soon as possible, by the formerly prisoner states of Eastern Europe. All this was to be expressed with great force in Mrs Thatcher's Bruges speech in September 1988 – a speech as deeply resented and opposed by her own FCO as it was by the professional Europeans in Brussels. Needless to say, her Foreign Secretary, Geoffrey Howe, was 'appalled'.

It was the looming threat of a single currency and EMU that most concerned Mrs Thatcher in the years before the Wall came down and, as a prelude to these further moves, the increasing pressure on her and the United Kingdom to bring sterling into the Exchange Rate Mechanism. On this matter, there was a fierce division between the views of No 10 and the then occupant of No 11, Nigel Lawson. Lawson, while sharing – indeed helping to shape – the Prime Minister's general monetarist policies came firmly to the view that the UK should join the ERM. He even convinced himself that, only by joining the ERM, could the UK successfully *resist* the single currency and the full list of requirements of the third phase of EMU.

Mrs Thatcher, who had inherited the policy of sterling outside the ERM from her predecessor, Jim Callaghan, had gone no further than to say that Britain would join only when 'the conditions were right' – a basically negative position, strongly endorsed by her own Economic Adviser, Alan Walters. The argument between the Downing Street neighbours grew evermore bitter when the Prime Minister discovered that her Chancellor had been shadowing the DMark, thus covertly but effectively joining the ERM with a fixed sterling-DMark parity.

3. *The Berlin Wall, Maastricht*

Matters came to a head on the eve of the June 1989 Madrid Summit of European leaders when Lawson and Howe threatened joint resignation unless the Prime Minister announced forthwith a date for sterling to enter the ERM. The Prime Minister conceded and reluctantly announced that the UK would join twelve months later. Howe was swiftly to pay the price for his conduct: his replacement at the FCO by the much more amenable and agreeable to Mrs Thatcher, John Major, and the transfer of the discontented Howe to the post of Leader of the House with the token emollient that he was henceforth to be the Deputy Prime Minister. Shortly after, a disappointed and frustrated Lawson resigned – to be succeeded by John Major as Chancellor and Major himself was replaced, after a very brief tenure at the FCO, by Douglas Hurd.

Mrs Thatcher, as the deadline for sterling's ERM entry approached, was still reluctant, but finally yielded to the joint pressures of her newly-appointed Chancellor John Major and Foreign Secretary Douglas Hurd. Having exacted one further condition – the abolition of controls on the movement of capital – from her EC partners, the UK on the eve of the Conservative Annual Conference in October 1990 at last made its – disastrous – decision to join.

At her last European Council meeting in Rome in October 1990, the Heads of Government agreed that phase two of EMU should begin in 1994. Only Britain voted against, the reasons stated by Mrs Thatcher with her resounding 'No, No, No' in the House of Commons on her return.

By this time of course the big issues of German reunification, Communist collapse and the extension of the European Treaties to embrace in principle, the security, foreign and defence policies of member states, had already emerged. Mrs Thatcher certainly had no enthusiasm for the coming together of the two Germanies but, having held with experts and Ministers a one-day Seminar at Chequers on the issues involved, concluded that the reunification was a fact of life that had to be accepted. Henceforth the admission to the European Community of the newly-liberated East European nations should be at the top of the agenda and further extensions of supranational power should be resisted.

The concept of checking the naked integrationism of Delors and his allies by adding to the EC what were planned to be two inter-governmental pillars, one for foreign and security policy, the other for legislation affecting immigration, asylum, police co-operation and Civil Law, *outside* the main body of the previous treaties, and thus excluding both the Brussels Commission and European Court of Justice, was part of the British response developed during Mrs Thatcher's remaining months as Prime Minister – months that were to be filled with the impact of other external events, the Iraqi invasion of Kuwait, preparations for the Gulf War and the demonstration yet again of the UK/US closeness and near-global rapport.

And then, Mrs Thatcher's eleven-year tenure of power was brought to its extraordinary and abrupt end in November 1990 by her own Cabinet. The resentful Geoffrey Howe resigned his unwanted job as Leader of the House of Commons and attacked the Prime Minister for her European policies in a brilliant resignation speech. This in turn triggered her long-term rival, Michael Heseltine, who had himself resigned as Defence Secretary over a helicopter purchase order in 1986 with strong overtones of Europe versus America as the UK's principal arms supplier, to announce his challenge as a candidate for the leadership. While unsuccessful in his own bid, Heseltine succeeded in inflicting sufficient damage on the Prime Minister to open the way, as the *tertium gaudens* in the subsequent contest, for John Major to enter No 10.

It fell then to John Major to undertake the crucial tasks of concluding the negotiations of this uniquely far-reaching and significant draft treaty – and of defending what was from the beginning a nearly-isolated Britain and her interests.

3. *The Berlin Wall, Maastricht*

In this task Major was entirely right to make the establishment of good personal relations with Chancellor Kohl his first priority. The chemistry between Mrs Thatcher and Kohl had not been good and the achievement of improved personal and political relations with Europe's now dominant figure was essential. The mistake Major made, to haunt him in the future, was to make during his visit to Germany the wrong-headed statement that he wanted to put Britain 'at the heart of Europe'. Wrong-headed, not only because that is simply not a realistic objective for any British government to pursue, but because on all the evidence Major himself did not for a moment seriously mean it – other than as a gesture of a genuine friendship and goodwill, in spite of his own and Britain's basic differences with its European neighbours.

As I write, in mid-2000, the general assessment of Major's 1990-7 Premiership could scarcely be less favourable, and in particular his alleged mishandling of the European issues and his own party in their ever-widening divisions on European policy. But, at least as far as the negotiations of the Maastricht Treaty go, Major's handling of the issues, was on the contrary, remarkably skilful and successful. His own account, in his autobiography, of the concluding Luxembourg and Hague European Councils that finalised the Maastricht Treaty, is itself a fascinating expose of the real as opposed to the Euro-mythical, world of bargaining and manoeuvring that underlies both the legislation and the Treaties of the European Union. It should be made compulsory reading for all UK Ministers saddled with future negotiating tasks.

Moreover on the crucial issues, against the flood tide of Euro enthusiasm (the Dutch draft treaty proclaimed, in terms, the 'federal destiny' of the Union – though wiser councils prevailed), he held on, and secured exemptions and opt-outs for the UK. The most crucial was undoubtedly the opt-out from phase three of Economic and Monetary Union, with its planned introduction of the single currency, the European Central Bank and treaty constraints on the extent of future government borrowing. The opt-out from these virtually irreversible commitments – although it did mean accepting the less onerous but still very unwelcome provisions of phase two of EMU – was indeed a success.

But there was more to come. The Europe-without-frontiers objective of the Commission and most of the other member states, were again resisted and are not to apply to the UK or to Eire. The frontiers are still far from secure but at least they can still be manned. The crucially important Common Foreign and Security Policy and its possible development into a Common Defence Policy as well, were brought into the treaty and the potential for their future expansion was, by that very fact – and as events were soon to demonstrate – created from the start. But at least all of this was made subject to initial voting unanimity and, by placing their provisions in a so-called Second Pillar of the treaty, the exclusion of the Brussels Commission and the European Court of Justice (ECJ) was secured. Finally and literally at the last minute – from the Thatcher-Conservative point of view a crucial prize – Major secured in the early hours of the last day a further exemption for the UK from the so-called Social Chapter – and its removal from the body of the treaty to the position of an attached protocol, from whose terms the UK was again excluded. Major was unwise to boast of 'Game, set and match' on his return to London, but to an informed and close Eurosceptic observer of the scene, his indeed was a considerable achievement. Moreover, it greatly assisted the new Prime Minister in uniting his Party and in winning the 1992 General Election.

Why then did it all go wrong and so quickly for Major? Within six months of election victory two unexpected events were to destroy the momentum of Maastricht itself – and to shatter the unity of the Conservative Party. The first was the Danish referendum on the Maastricht Treaty, when that remarkable and courageous electorate voted 'No' in June 1992. The Second Reading of the European Community's Bill, to enact the Maastricht Treaty, had already sailed through the House of Commons, with a me-too Labour Party under its then new Leader John Smith finding little to object to. The committee stage was about to begin but, since European treaties must be unanimously approved by member states, further progress on the bill had to be halted. Meanwhile desperate efforts were mounted – with the UK and John Major just starting their six-months-term in the Presidency much involved – to find a mixture of bribes, threats and verbal formulae that would enable an embarrassed Danish government to return to its electors with at least a fig leaf of concession to help change their votes. This process was not to be completed until November 1992 and meanwhile the bill was stalled.

Then fortune struck again. The disastrous consequences of sterling imprisoned in the Exchange Rate Mechanism at a plus or minus 6 per cent rate against the DMark and the other Euro currencies, with its clearly recorded damage to the UK in terms of rising unemployment, a widening trade deficit, and a mounting total of bankruptcies, led, predictably, to a run on the pound and the need, under the ERM rules, to sustain the exchange rate by intervening in the currency markets. The outward flow of foreign money from London became a flood, yet no collective European rescue attempt was mounted. The bank rate was hoisted to 15 per cent and the nation's gold and dollar reserves were savagely depleted. Norman Lamont, the Chancellor, appeared outside the Treasury building, on the pavement of Great George Street, as the pound was jerked free from the ERM. To the government, 14 September 1992 was *Black* Wednesday, but to the critics and opponents of ERM and still more of EMU and the Maastricht Treaty, it was *White* Wednesday.

Combined with the Danish referendum, this was a massive blow to the central economic policy of the government, to the notion of fixed exchange rates and to the EMU/single currency proposals that lay, along with foreign and security policies, at the heart of the Maastricht Treaty.

When and as the bill's committee stage resumed on the floor of the House of Commons, two rather remarkable processes took place. first, with democracy now alert, a detailed examination of both the content and the implications of the Maastricht Treaty took place. And second as part of that process the conversion of the majority of the government's own supporters in the Conservative Parliamentary Party from passive if unenthusiastic Europhiles, into reluctant but seriously worried Eurosceptics. Even with the covert assistance of the Labour Front Bench which limited its opposition to the Treaty to the exclusion from it of the Social Chapter and which, with the government's enthusiastic co-operation, agreed to timetable the crucial EMU debates into the early hours of the morning, with the Press Gallery empty and the BBC in bed, the process of conversion and discovery could not be stopped. Indeed with a small majority and a handful of backbench MPs in open revolt, the bill itself was on occasions at risk. Moreover the increasingly Eurosceptic view of the Conservative Party was undoubtedly heard – or shared – in the Cabinet itself, some of whose members were, notoriously, to be dubbed by an off-guard but exasperated Prime Minister as the 'bastards'.

All of this obviously increased Major's problems of Party management, made in some ways all the more difficult because in his own views the Prime Minister leant more towards the Eurosceptic than to the Europhile wing in his Party. Indeed, having read the former Prime Minister's Autobiography, that conclusion really is inescapable as these passages on Maastricht demonstrate: it 'had been a fork in the road. Our partners wanted a single currency. We did not. They wanted a Social Chapter. We did not. They wanted more harmonisation of policy. We did not. They wanted more Community control of defence. We did not. Increasingly, they talked in private of a federal destination, even though in public they were reassuring about a Europe of Nation States'. Many other passages point to the same conclusion – a fundamental difference of aim and objective between Britain and most other EU member states. And those differences were fortified by Major's strong dislike of Commission President Delors whose 'hypocrisy and hectoring enraged him', Mitterand whom he found to be aloof and ill-informed, particularly on economic questions and the whole modus operandi of Council and Commission where Kohl, Mitterand and Delors so clearly and arrogantly ruled the roost.

But Major had negotiated and signed the treaty with its substantial UK opt-outs and so he had to see it through the House of Commons. Nevertheless, the hardening Conservative position in the years after the Maastricht Treaty received Parliamentary assent was reflected even more clearly in the government's White Paper, a *Europe of Nation States*. Its main purpose was to make clear the government's opposition to any further supranational initiatives; in particular to those that were beginning to emerge from yet another IGC and which were to be adopted in the Amsterdam Treaty only weeks after the 1997 General Election. The purpose of the new treaty was of course to carry still further forward the giant steps taken at Maastricht five years before. With strong Franco-German support, a large new framework for future security, foreign policy and defence was to be given treaty authority and much of the content of the so-called Third Pillar – dealing with civil law, free movement of people, immigration and asylum – was to be transferred into the central structure of the Rome Treaty, and thus brought within the competencies of the Brussels Commission and the European Court of Justice. Among its most striking features was the so-called Stability and Growth Pact which authorised – once the single currency had been launched – the imposition by the Commission and the Council of heavy fines on any member state which allowed its annual borrowing requirement to exceed the 3 per cent GDP limit, as laid down in the Maastricht Treaty.

Most of these and other moves to change and extend the provisions for majority voting in the Council of Ministers were, if the Major government's White Paper was to be believed, destined to be opposed by the UK (although, oddly, the Stability Pact was absent from the White Paper's coverage, presumably on the grounds that, as long as the UK retained its opt-out from the EMU, we would be unaffected by its provisions).

Curiously, it was in events occurring outside these IGC negotiations and well after the much disputed Maastricht Treaty and implementing bill went through that Major seemed to play his cards clumsily, failing to satisfy either wing of his divided Party, and gaining no ground or respect in Europe. His insistence on maintaining the 'blocking minority' in the Council of Ministers at the same numerical level as it had been *after* Sweden, Austria and Finland had entered the European Union was unconvincing and not thought through; the blocking of Belgium's Prime Minister Dehaene as Delors' successor as President of the Brussels Commission – only to replace him by the equally federalist Santer from Luxembourg – was simply pointless. But in no issue did the government more stupidly open itself for attack than on the outbreak of BSE in the UK's livestock industry and the ban on UK beef exports to Europe that inevitably ensued. This was the last issue on which the UK could rightly or convincingly threaten with an 'empty chair'.

It was these badly-judged moves that allowed the Labour Party, under its Europhile leaders, both to deceive itself and the country that Britain's basic problems in Europe were not the fundamentally different goals that most of our Continental neighbours and ourselves were almost bound to pursue. Instead, according to Labour's spin doctors, they were due wholly to an outbreak of xenophobia in the Tory Right Wing and the populist press, with government policy towards Europe either in a state of paralysis or driven to reflect the hostility now rampant in the Conservative Party.

The Major government was to last for almost its full five-year term before the May 1997 election. Europe became an increasing problem not only because of genuine differences and avoidable blunders in the Major government's dealings with the European Union but also because of the ever-increasing divisions within the Party on the issues involved. During the same period in the Labour Party, policy during the short-lived leadership of John Smith who was elected after Kinnock's resignation in 1992, was strongly Europhile. John Smith himself, during the period when he had been Shadow Chancellor, had welcomed the UK's entry to the ERM. The UK's forced withdrawal in September 1992, largely escaped Labour Front Bench attack. John Smith was not allowed the time needed to really develop his overall policies for the future but, on what evidence there is, he seemed to adhere to a kind of three-tier vision of future government affecting the UK, in which the powers of Edinburgh and Brussels were marked for major expansion and that of London and Westminster to be substantially reduced.

It was however Smith's successor, Tony Blair, who did most to place Europe in the centre stage of British politics. In the less than three-year period that Blair was Leader of the Opposition before the May 1997 General Election, winning that election, whenever it came, was understandably his overwhelming preoccupation and aim. After four successive general election defeats, it was easy for the new Leader to persuade himself that any unpopular baggage in terms of inherited party policies and attitudes had to be abandoned. New policies, including Europe, had to be handled with great care and with a very sensitive regard to public opinion – and for the opinion of the media. As part of this strategy, it is now very clear that reaching an understanding with the Eurosceptic press magnate,

Rupert Murdoch, and if possible the editorial support of both the *Sun* and the *Times* newspapers were highly prized, even essential aims.

His own Europhile convictions had therefore to be held on a tight rein. As I have asserted in the introduction, the 1997 Labour Manifesto was objectively dishonest. What was not dishonest, but which had the advantage of being both popular and democratic, was the pledge to hold a referendum if a future Labour government decided to abandon Major's opt-out from the single currency. It would therefore not abandon sterling without the consent of the British people. In the event, such was the size of the May 1997 Labour victory that it is doubtful whether the Labour Party needed to make any such concession to popular opinion. But that decision was of course to be one of the central issues for the Blair government throughout the period of government that followed – the issues which will undoubtedly greatly influence attitudes at the next General Election and in the Parliament that will follow.

The immediate issue awaiting the incoming Labour government was of course the conclusion of the IGC, the final stage of what was to become the Amsterdam Treaty. And there, bursting with goodwill and energy, and echoing again and again his intention to place himself and his country 'at the heart of Europe', Blair duly arrived only five weeks after entering Downing Street and agreed the new treaty of Amsterdam. There was little that he needed to do. The European partners were delighted to be joined by a man whom they judged to be an enthusiast for integration and they were certainly not going to demand last-minute and politically embarrassing concessions from the UK. His immediate lifting of the British veto on the Social Chapter and the UK's acceptance of it was enough for the day. And the wary and the critical back home were satisfied with the new treaty's statement that, in the developing defence policy, nothing should be imposed upon those states that looked to their security in their membership of NATO. The new government was not opposed to the single currency – and didn't even raise the Stability Pact issues – but was allowed, without challenge, to consider the hows and whens of joining.

Not quite John Major's post-Maastricht 'Game, set and match' but a most excellent and promising beginning. Since then of course a number of major developments have raised issues of the most complex, serious and divisive nature: the development of a European Defence Policy, starting with the Franco-German meeting in December 1997 and Blair's St Malo meeting with President Chirac a few weeks later – well before the events in Kosovo and all that has developed since; the thrust towards a massive enlargement of membership of the European Union; and the actual launch of the single currency, the Euro, and the completion of the third phase of EMU for the eleven states, including France and Germany, which now comprise Euroland.

The first two issues face Britain and Europe with major decisions – decisions that could well be taken by the end of 2000 or a little later on. They deserve separate analysis and treatment and are dealt with at some length in chapters 5 and 7 of Part II that follow. The single currency, since its adoption by the eleven has already taken place and because preparations and debate are already well advanced in the UK, can be more appropriately covered in the remaining part of this chapter which seeks only to bring up-to-the-present the story of Britain and Europe.

The single currency issue has been a source of continuing and growing embarrassment for the Blair government. Like Mrs Thatcher's joining the ERM when 'the conditions were right' or when 'the time is ripe', joining the single currency when sufficient 'convergence' of the British and European economies has taken place, is a policy without a timetable and without a real commitment. Chancellor Gordon Brown's statement in November 1997 of the five tests that the economy must pass before entry settled nothing: the five tests are too imprecise for that and any judgement about their achievement – or non-achievement – is predominantly subjective. But is that why that statement was made? Is the government simply following a wait-and-see policy that has far more to do with public opinion and the Murdoch press than it has to do with any objective economic criteria? That devoted Europhile, Lord Jenkins, a welcome and not infrequent visitor to No 10, clearly thinks so: and while he is almost part of the New Labour establishment, he has allowed his exasperation a public airing, complaining in the *Independent* of 'lack of courage', of that old failure to grasp nettles, with which all in political life are familiar. More importantly, this is the view increasingly held in Brussels and in the other capitals of Europe where enthusiasm for Blair seems distinctly on the wane.

On the other hand, are not the Prime Minister and his Chancellor simply being realistic? Surely their Europhile credentials and general enthusiasm for things European are strong enough for the world to give them the benefit of the doubt. And is not their announced decision to spend not tens, but hundreds of millions of pounds in preparation for the conversion of government accounts and payment systems to the euro, strong evidence of their intent? The former Lib-Dem Leader, Paddy Ashdown, hailed the announcement of their pre-entry expenditure as 'a crossing of the Rubicon'. But it is quite clear that no decision will be made in this Parliament and there are differently nuanced views among Cabinet Ministers as to when, earlier or later – or if at all – it should be made in the next.

The truth is that the government is faced with a dilemma that may well prove to be insoluble. For their underlying problem is that the case for Britain abandoning sterling and adopting the single currency is, on merit, almost ludicrously weak.

In the light of all past experience, not to mention simple common sense, there are and must be obvious problems in imposing a single bank rate, interest rate and monetary policy on some 350 million people, living in the widely different economic conditions of Portugal and Greece at one extreme and Germany and The Netherlands at the other. A continental 'one-size' bank rate as now imposed on Euroland by the European Central Bank in Frankfurt simply does not fit the varying needs of stimulus and restraint in so diverse an area. Even within a country as homogeneous as our own, significant regional differences in economic conditions between North and South make a single currency and a single bank rate tolerable *only* because of central government spending and the promotion of strong regional policies to assist our less prosperous areas. But if Newcastle-on-Tyne sometimes finds it difficult to live with London, how much more unlikely are Athens, Dublin, Paris, The Hague and London itself to benefit from a uniform interest rate, laid down by the European Central Bank?

Then there is another equally unanswerable objection to a single currency and to a single bank rate policy: over time, the growth of productivity and competitiveness in different countries and regions become increasingly disparate, with the tendency for economic growth and activity to concentrate in some countries (and regions), generating still more inward investment, while slow growth, then stagnation, then recession hits other countries (or regions). How then can a country, which no longer has its own currency or its own central bank restore its competitiveness – as we and other countries can do today by lowering our exchange rates with appropriate adjustments in our interest rate and monetary policies?

Without these instruments of policy, countries are left with semi-stagnation and rising unemployment, large-scale emigration of workers and their families to where the jobs are in Continental Europe; or accepting substantial cuts in wages and salaries to improve competitiveness. No one in their senses would wish to be faced with such unattractive choices.

Further, what governments are banned from doing is to stimulate their own economies by increasing domestic demand through increased public borrowing. All this reflects the monetarist dogmas of the 1980s and the almost paranoid fears of *inflation* when the emerging global economic problem, increasingly powered by the transparency of the itnernet, is clearly the old enemy *deflation*. The Maastricht Treaty has virtually written deflation into the treaty itself, with its rigid ceilings on the total quantity of national debt, its on-going 3 per cent ceiling on annual government borrowing and its insistence on balanced budgets over the economic cycle as a whole.

To sum it up: joining the single currency and phase three of EMU involves not only the abolition of our own currency, the pound sterling, the turning of the Bank of England into a branch bank of the European Central Bank (ECB) in Frankfurt and the surrender to that Bank of a substantial part of our national gold, dollar and other currency reserves, but it commits us to the imposition of treaty constraints, enforced by heavy fines, on the annual amount that our government is allowed to borrow.

I would hesitate to express myself so strongly but for the fact that I know my assessment is shared not just by most economists and businessmen who have turned their minds seriously to the question of the single currency, but that my main worries continue to be articulated by no less an authority than the present Governor of the Bank of England, Eddie George. In his very carefully considered Churchill Memorial lecture delivered in Luxembourg on 21 February 1995, Mr George had this to say about the consequences of joining a single currency without full convergence, or competitiveness, being achieved: 'There really are only two possible adjustment mechanisms – neither of which on present evidence looks likely to be particularly effective. First there is the possibility of migration from areas of high unemployment to areas of lower unemployment ... secondly there could be pressure for large fiscal transfers from countries with lower unemployment to countries where unemployment was higher. Neither of these possibilities is particularly attractive. Either long-term stagnation in some countries or the rapid expansion of these adjustment mechanisms could become the source of political as well as economic disharmony within Europe ...'

It is also worth recalling the words of the Chancellor's own long-time economic adviser and confidant, now the government's official Chief Economic Adviser, Mr Ed Balls. In a Fabian pamphlet published in December 1992, a year after the Maastricht Treaty had been negotiated, but before the Growth and Stability Pact had taken shape, Mr Balls had this to say both about the policies and institutions shortly to be introduced and the underlying monetarist doctrines that informed them: 'The economic implications of the Maastricht Treaty are dangerous and unworkable. Labour's current European policy – early re-entry into the ERM and support for the Maastricht Treaty provision for a single currency during the course of this decade – risks contradicting what should be Europe and Labour's underlying aim: a stable, growing, low-unemployment community'.

Mr Balls then spelt out some of the costs: 'There would also be costs to EMU; and these costs – in terms of unemployment and slow growth – would prove to be prohibitively high. EMU means that no country can run a different monetary policy and have a different interest rate from that set by the European Central Bank'. And as for the underlying monetarist obsession with inflation that informs all these arrangements, he has this to say: 'A monetarist policy of trying to pursue low inflation through high interest rates and an overvalued exchange rate ... is economically destabilising and politically unsustainable'.

I doubt whether Mr Balls, generally Europhile as he certainly is, has wholly abandoned these views – anymore than has the Governor of the Bank of England his. So, with the additional authority of the two Eddies behind me, I simply reaffirm the negative verdict on the whole single currency-ECB venture. And my critique has little or nothing to do with the marked depreciation of the exchange rate of the euro, which unfortunately has pre-empted serious discussion of the impact within Euroland itself of the single currency and which has been allowed to inflict such damage on UK exporters.

All this leaves unanswered one crucial question. If the case against is so strong and so clear, why on earth have the governments and peoples of Euroland undertaken this extraordinary enterprise? The answer is that a number of the Euro States are indeed aware of the considerable problems that already face – and continue to face – their economies by adopting the single currency. Their eyes have been, if not wide open, certainly not closed. The member states do indeed have very different economic structures and there are large differences between the competitiveness and sophistication of the different national economies. Simply to come within the two minimum requirements – an annual government borrowing requirement of not more than 3 per cent of GDP and an overall national debt not larger than 60 per cent of GDP – has, over the past several years obliged many of the Euroland eleven to cut public expenditure, to raise taxation, and to operate tight monetary policies in order to become eligible for membership. And the overall effect has been to wipe out any prospect of economic recovery in the whole decade of the 1990s. The European Union that began with the high level of unemployment in 1992 of 9.2 per cent, ended in 1999 with the same high percentage figure. During that period, the UK has substantially reduced its unemployment total while Germany increased its from 6.6 to 9.1 per cent, France from 10.4 to 11 per cent, and Italy from 8.8 to 11.3 per cent. The total number of people registered unemployed in the European Union stands today not far below the 17 million mark that has been recorded during most of the last decade. The depreciation of the euro since its launch on 1 January 1999 has been helpful to the economy of the area – although damaging to the UK whose supine Chancellor has done nothing to influence downwards the exchange rate of the pound – restoring some much-needed competitiveness to German and French exports and this should continue in the year ahead.

But for the governments of the eleven, economic gain from forming the single currency is not and was not the point. Indeed, only the deranged could believe that Chancellor Kohl and the German Bundesbank abandoned the DMark for reasons of economic gain. Of course they didn't, it was for the achievement of political union that they sacrificed the DMark – and the quotations I have already deployed show that that is the purpose not only of Kohl and his successor German government, but of nearly all the governments of Europe.

It is this political gain, with Germany and France in the lead, with Brussels cheering them on and federalists in Italy, Holland, Belgium, Luxembourg and Spain clapping their hands, that has produced something like euphoria in Euroland. The launch of the single currency is seen by them to be a massive leap towards the ever-closer union, the political union and the ultimate goal of a state, the United States of Europe. That is the spur and the achievement

Indeed the governments of the eleven know very well that while the single currency and EMU are immense integrationist achievements, they can only be staging posts on the road to a complete political union. Having lost their own macro-economic powers to influence exchange rates and interest rates, it will be essential that at the European level, new measures are devised and new policy instruments forged to take their place. Of these, the equipment of the Commission with greatly enhanced powers to raise taxes, undertake loans and spend revenues are leading contenders, with tax harmonisation already high on the European agenda.

What makes the British government's stance in fact farcical and for our European partners deeply suspect is that the British government alone denies that there is any serious political or constitutional issue involved that the euro is not above all about a major transfer of the powers of government, but is simply a matter of the balance between the pluses and minuses of a wholly economic calculation. In this, they haven't even persuaded their own Governor of the Bank of England, Eddie George. The Governor is indeed at the very heart of the British establishment and the last person to express immoderate views, particularly when they are not those of the Chancellor and the Prime Minister. But in a speech to the Leeds and Bradford Chamber of Commerce on 11 April 2000 honesty compelled him to say: 'Monetary Union is fundamentally a political rather than economic issue ... it necessarily involves the deliberate pooling of national sovereignty over important aspects of public policy ...'

So, the Governor too joins that long list of European and world leaders who cannot bring themselves to lie about the political implications of abandoning your own currency.

One can understand only too well why the government and British Europhiles are so stubborn in maintaining their pretence. One *certain* consequence of Britain's abandoning its own currency and the control of its own interest rates and money supply, and of transferring those powers to European institutions, is a massive reduction in the power of our own electorate, of our own democracy. Today, the Prime Minister, the Chancellor of the Exchequer and all their colleagues can be dismissed – and will be – if the majority of the people dislike the policies they are pursuing. If for example unemployment is unacceptably high, if interest and mortgage rates are set at penal levels, if the pattern and volume of public expenditure is judged to be wrong or unfair, then the government, by the end of its five-year span, will be dismissed and replaced by those pledged to different and corrective actions.

But if these corrective actions are no longer available to any British government, if policies are made and executed by unelected bankers in Frankfurt, unelected officials in Brussels, by near-immutable treaties enforced and interpreted by unelected judges in Strasbourg and Luxembourg, or even by majority voting in the fifteen-member Council of Ministers, that is the end of democracy itself. Nor can the legitimacy of our own Westminster Parliament be somehow replaced by that bogus Assembly, the so-called European Parliament, in which Britain has only 65 out of over 600 seats.

To sum up, if the economic case for the single currency is feeble and unconvincing, the political and constitutional consequences of EMU and the Euro are utterly unacceptable.

A substantial debate on the euro and whether the UK should abolish the pound sterling and join it has already taken place here in Britain. As it has developed, not only have important economic groupings – the Institute of Directors, the Small Business Federation – moved strongly into opposition, but public opinion too, as frequently held opinion polls reveal, is increasingly hostile to the project, with well over 60 per cent against.

Indeed, the evidence is that having now lost the economic argument, the government has, at least for a period, abandoned it. The organisation set up by the government, with prominent opposition Europhiles, the CBI and others, to press the case for the single currency, *Britain in Europe*, has been obliged by the government itself to cease and desist – and instead, to argue the very different case for the United Kingdom remaining in the European Union itself. It appears to be the government's calculation that its best hope of getting the single currency adopted is to persuade the electorate that to reject it would mean leaving the European Union itself.

This is not the place to discuss the tactics and techniques of persuasion, legitimate or otherwise, which I have deliberately separated from the main argument of the book and have placed separately in the Introduction. But if the argument about the euro has been more or less suspended, it is far from over. And of one thing we can be certain. In the very end, in the privacy of the voting booth, it will be the people of Britain who will decide whether they wish to keep or surrender their own currency – and with it much of their own independence and their own democracy.

Part II

4

Alternative Futures

The disadvantages to the UK of embracing the euro currency and the still further steps towards European economic and political integration that it has already set in train are not difficult to argue and assert. But the big question that has emerged is not about the merits, or rather demerits, of joining the single currency but about whether these are not burdens that the British now have to bear; that Britain has run out of options; that membership of the euro and with it ever-closer union are inevitable. No two words are more frequently on the lips of the Europhiles than 'isolated' and 'marginalised' – the dreaded fate that will await us if we dared to stay outside; and, underlying so much of it, the assertion that, stripped of empire, we are now no more than a middle-sized European nation that must run with the pack. To this, the grander Europhiles like to add a hint of 'manifest destiny' and of historical inevitability.

It would be dangerous to dismiss the persuasive power of these concepts. One of the great strengths of the now defunct Marxist-Leninist creed, that which gave it – apart from Soviet armed might – such widespread appeal and potency was the claim that history decreed the outcome; that victory for Communism and defeat for its capitalist adversary were inevitable. Nothing so disarms a protagonist in a struggle as the sense of impending defeat. In the ongoing debate on Britain and Europe in the seven years since the Maastricht Treaty was signed, opinion polls have consistently shown a majority – a growing majority – *against* abandoning the pound sterling and adopting the Euro – and at the same time, in spite of the pledge made by all three political parties of a referendum on the issue, a majority view is constantly expressed that we are *bound* to join.

The Europhiles have not won the argument, but have they undermined and sapped the self confidence of the British people to the point where we are ready to cave in?

I think not. But the half-buried assumptions that help feed this defeatism need to be exposed and challenged. And so too do the reasons and assumptions made by those who proclaim our 'European destiny' and who believe that our immersion into the European Union is not only inevitable but right.

There are of course many streams of thought and experience that join together in promoting the cause of an 'ever-closer' European Union. Among these – the most appealing – are the memories of war: the almost unbearable tragedy of 1914-18 and the sheer horror of the war of conquest and extermination that Nazi Germany inflicted on the whole Continent from 1939 to 1945. If indeed, as some of our strongest integrationists still claim, European integration was the only way to prevent yet another tragedy, the appeal would be too powerful to resist. For France and Germany's geographical neighbours it was precisely these considerations that helped launch the original European enterprise in the late 1940s and, while it has less potency now, it still retains a strong appeal. But for the United Kingdom, while far from opposing the increasing integration between Germany and its neighbours, the stronger and more acceptable strategy for avoiding future wars and ensuring peace in Europe has been the absorption of German military power, together with that of most other European states, in the American-commanded NATO alliance to which virtually the whole of Western Europe has belonged since the treaty was signed in 1949.

There are other reasons, expectations and hopes, that drive

forward the Europhiles. The argument for doing things in concert with others and thus increasing the UK's collective influence and power is bound to weigh heavily with both our political elite and with their permanent professional advisers – the diplomats in the Foreign Office. But those considerations are the classic arguments for alliances and for treaties, not for the uniquely integrationist, supranational institutions and commitments of the European Union. More importantly Prime Minister Macmillan, the man who made the first and unsuccessful attempt to take Britain into the Common Market, and his successor, Edward Heath, who succeeded a decade later, were undoubtedly motivated by their sense of the decline of British power and of the economic strength that sustains it and the contrasting experience on the Continent where a great surge of growth and prosperity in the 1950s and 1960s was taking place. Ironically, that great surge came to its end in the very year, 1973, of Britain's entry – and it has not returned. This of course has been one of the factors that has helped produce the markedly different Conservative Leadership of today which, together with the majority of Conservatives in both Parliament and the country is opposed to still further integration and would wish to see at least some repatriation of powers previously transferred to Brussels.

The main driving force now for further integration into Europe is the Labour government and New Labour Party of Prime Minister Tony Blair. What then are the arguments and considerations that underlie Labour's enthusiasm, almost a passion for Europe?

Judging by both their public statements and their actions, the Labour Leadership holds strongly the view that the UK has no alternative, that we must be at the heart of Europe, never isolated and whenever possible giving Leadership to our partners and to the European Union. To be anything other than Europhile in the integrationist sense is to jeopardise jobs and prosperity, to be blindly isolationist or, worse, to be an extremist, a xenophobe. The UK's

113

previous difficulties with its Continental neighbours, as rehearsed in a previous chapter, have been almost wholly due to either Mrs Thatcher's stridency, John Major's feebleness, or divisions within the Conservative Party.

It is difficult to take these assertions seriously. For the most part it is on the surface, the knock-about of traditional Party politics, and events are likely to make it increasingly difficult to sustain. As the Prime Minister and his ministerial colleagues are beginning to discover, desperate as they are not to be the odd man out, isolation on European issues on many occasions cannot be avoided.

But, as with so much in human affairs, there are deeper, half-hidden impulses and assumptions far more cogent than their more frequently stated reasons, that propel Labour's Leadership and its Liberal bedfellows to the goal of ever-closer union.

One of the most potent is the almost hypnotic spell that 'globalisation' exerts on the thoughts and policies of New Labour. We live, they constantly tell each other, in a wholly new world, in a new century and in a new millennium. All previous history is irrelevant, all existing institutions are out of date. Above all, the power of global capitalism is what is now the dominant force in national and international affairs.

Globalisation is a large concept with many component parts. It certainly includes the immense increase in world trade, both between the advanced developed economies and with the growing new tiger economies in what were previously underdeveloped countries. It has much to do too with the revolutionary changes in information technology, joining people and institutions together worldwide in almost instantaneous contact. It is perhaps best exemplified by the internet, that free and unregulated zone for information exchange and personal contact, open to all, worldwide, who can access it. And at its very centre, there is the free movement of money, of capital and the felt presence of the multinational, giant corporation. In this global economy, massive movements of money are constantly taking place as corporate and individual speculators look for short-term gain in buying and selling currencies, bonds and equities. And alongside them, the finance department managers of large firms restlessly seek mergers and acquisitions and endlessly examine the advantages of making new investment, in one country rather than another.

Few Blair or Brown speeches are complete without some reference to the need to take account of these towering forces – *and to do nothing that would in any way offend their controllers.* And so there has to be a great assault on the policies, traditions, institutions and beliefs that have helped shape our national life and the outlook of our people. To face these new challenges and to cope with these giant forces, we must modernise.

And how they revel in their near-helplessness. How they almost gloat over the now dwarfed and puny state which they have been elected to govern. Above all, how irrelevant in a global economy the nation state has now become.

So, in the great debate about the British and the European Union, there can be no such thing as loss of UK sovereignty, of surrendering powers to unelected institutions like the European Commission in Brussels or the European Bank in Frankfurt. Why? because power has long since departed our shores, swallowed up in the great maw of the now global economy.

So, they say, there is not much at stake in ceasing to have a separate currency, in scrapping the pound sterling, in joining the euro. We may first have to adjust our economy, to bring it more closely in line with those on mainland Europe but beyond that there is nothing to lose. A separate currency with its own exchange rate is no longer an asset; it is at best useless, at worst a target for speculative attack.

And the same is true of the Central Bank, of the Bank of England which, with varying degrees of government involvement, still decides the UK's interest rate policy. Decides? Not in the global economy. It is the rates set by other financial centres, together with the judgement of the world markets that determine interest rates and their differentials. So why not hand over bank rate and monetary policy to the European Bank in Frankfurt? And how in a global economy can any government fail to cut and cut again its corporation and business taxes in order to retain – and attract – its multinational corporations, and how can it permit its personal income tax rates and its death duties to be higher than those in other attractive locations, if it wishes to avoid the flight of the rich?

Of course there is something in all this. The embrace of globalisation on the world economy would not be so intense if it were not. But while it is true that the old strategies of state regulation and control developed during the Second World War are now largely ineffective, the present emphasis on the hegemony of the global economy and of market capitalism is massively overstated. It is of course a heaven-sent excuse not just for failure to rectify injustices and to meet serious needs, but for not even trying to alter the underlying relationships of wealth and power.

Certainly, real problems for effective macro-economic policy exist. Nations cannot control and fix at will their currency exchange rates – and that indeed is one of the consequences of the globalisation of capital. But that is the basic case for floating, rather than fixed, exchange rates – the system that the world has adopted since the early 1970s. But exchange rates – provided that a nation still has a currency of it own to exchange – can indeed be *influenced* by government measures: and no instrument is more powerful in doing that than the bank rate/interest rates that are set. If interest rates in London are substantially higher than in Continental and other financial centres, and inflation rates broadly similar, speculative short-term capital will flow strongly into the City to buy sterling assets – and this will push up the exchange rate of the pound. Again, if London rates are significantly lower than in other centres, then speculative money will leave London for the higher rewards available elsewhere. They will therefore sell sterling and the sterling exchange rate will fall.

In refuting the Europhile assertion that the nation state, in terms of macro-economic policies, has been totally enfeebled, the metaphor of the ship of state can be usefully employed. Globalisation and the power of the global economy can be likened to the ocean, with its immense power and ever-changing moods. But the vessels that sail upon it are not, if they are properly constructed, to be smashed or sunk by even the strongest waves. And, like an ocean-going vessel, the ship of state travels successfully from point A to point B, reaches its harbour and delivers its cargoes and passengers in spite of all the force of wind and tide. In two words, the ship of state like a vessel at sea has to *steer* and to *navigate*. Economic policy today is an exercise in steering and navigation – not control – and, providing the crew know what they are about and the vessel is soundly constructed, they need not fear the crossing, however rough the sea.

Of course national control over interest rates can be exercised unwisely as well as wisely. There is indeed a still open question about our present Chancellor's decision – much applauded as it has been in financial and political circles – to transfer the power to decide our own bank rate to the Governor of the Bank of England and his Monetary Policy Committee. But, that apart, the Chancellor has given the Governor and his Committee extremely restrictive terms of reference in exercising their new authority. They have to give overriding importance to containing inflation below a two-and-a-half per cent per annum ceiling, regardless of other major considerations such as the competitiveness of the exchange rate and levels of demand in the economy. And, of course, at the time of making this decision, the present Chancellor was strongly influenced by his desire to prepare the way – and signal to Brussels and Frankfurt that the UK is really committed – to handing over these key controls to the European Central Bank.

If globalisation provides Labour's Europhiles with a seemingly powerful intellectual argument not only for the single currency but for still deeper integration with the European Union, it is strongly reinforced – though this is seldom directly expressed – by the driving force of emotion and argument that combine in their rejection of the nation state. For if the nation state is now held to be virtually useless in dealing with a globalised economy, it is still held to be responsible for most of the horrors – war, tyranny and persecution – of the century that has just ended. Alongside this there has long existed a rather elitist and class-conscious cultural preference for things European and their own 'severance from the culture of the country' among leaders of the Liberal and Labour parties. As Orwell put it in his great 1940 essay, The Lion and the Unicorn: 'In intention at any rate, the English intelligentsia are Europeanised. They take their cookery from Paris and their opinions from Moscow. In the general patriotism of the country they form a sort of island of dissident thought. England is perhaps the only great country whose intellectuals are ashamed of their own nationality'.

Today, had he still been alive, I suspect George Orwell would have repeated his critique in a slightly amended text: 'In intention at any rate, the English intelligentsia are Europeanised. They take their cookery from Paris, their holidays in Tuscany and their opinions from Brussels. In the general patriotism of the country they form a sort of island of dissident thought'.

But the rejection of the nation state and the loyalties which it invokes has a far more serious genesis than the cultural elitism that Orwell attacked. More than anything else, it was a product of the First World War and the reflection of decent men and women, in all classes, of the horrors of those events. Tremendous, almost unbelievable courage and dogged commitment were shown by millions and millions of ordinary men – French, German, Italian, Russian as well British and Commonwealth – during the slaughter of those four years

– a courage and sacrifice called forth by unquestioned allegiance to the nation state. For many of that generation and the one that followed it, the conviction formed that the First World War should never have happened and, if its start could not be prevented, then peace should have been negotiated years before the final German collapse. If the sovereignty of the nation state and the loyalty of its citizens, some argued, leads to such international conflict and destruction, then that loyalty and sovereignty should be abandoned and superseded by an international rule of law.

In the democracies, certainly post-1918, aggressive nationalism, and over-assertive claims on others, were disciplined and rebuked. Indeed the dominant post-war mood was one of 'never again', and of neo-pacificism. Unhappily this was not the mood of the strongest defeated power, Germany. The Weimar Republic collapsed under the weight of economic failure and the fierce vengeful chauvinism and racial hatred of Hitler's Nazi Party.

Among the British Left, these were also the years when Marxist doctrines exercised very considerable influence. The First World War itself, followed barely a decade after the guns fell silent by the economic catastrophe of the Great Slump, not only imposed tragedy and hardship on tens of millions of people across the globe, but loosened their loyalties to traditional institutions. Above all, as people searched for some explanation of these catastrophic events, and for some means of avoiding their reoccurrence, the Marxist-Leninist analysis of the contradictions of capitalism – the competitive struggle for profits and markets, the national rivalries and imperial quests that they gave rise to – was widely circulated and had for many a highly persuasive plausibility. And if, on this analysis, capitalism was the root cause of unemployment and war, surely all the capitalist states were to blame and the only hope for civilisation and peace lay in the repudiation of capitalism, in the new order pioneered by Lenin and Stalin in Soviet Russia and in the message that the workers of the world must unite to overthrow the bourgeois state everywhere.

It was not only the Left intellectuals who responded to this analysis, but virtually the whole high command of the pre-war Labour Party. As war approached in the late 1930s, Labour's Leader, Clem Attlee, opposed the desperately late efforts of the Chamberlain government to re-arm – including the introduction of national service – on the grounds that the UK was itself a capitalist-imperialist state and therefore not to be trusted with enhanced military power. At the same time, Attlee was openly supporting and encouraging the recruitment of British volunteers to the International Brigade to fight Franco and Fascism in the Spanish Civil War. And Sir Stafford Cripps, at that stage admittedly very far Left indeed, was telling Spitfire workers in 1937: 'You have the most glorious opportunity that the workers have ever had – refuse to make ammunitions, refuse to make armaments'.

The Second World War ended all that, but no one can doubt that, during the long years of the Cold War against communism that ensued, the Labour Left was slow indeed to recognise that the Soviet Union was a threat to world peace and that the 'capitalist' West, led by capitalist America, was not the real aggressor.

New Labour has of course no problem with capitalism. But it has, with its mantra about inclusiveness and non-discrimination, its own particular hang-ups. Above all, the nation state with its anthem, its flag, its exclusiveness and its frontier stands for all those conservative and historical things that awaken memories of a guilt-laden national past and which its Leader, the Prime Minister, so ardently wishes to abjure. Of course there is strong argument for devolution and decentralisation of decision-making in the UK, but New Labour cannot recognise that the downside is a fragmentation and a weakening of the nation as a whole. And again, with the transfer of powers to Europe, New Labour cannot comprehend that the projects of 'ever-closer' union and the single currency have tremendous implications for our independence as a separate sovereign state.

Paradoxically, the denigration of the nation state, so essential to the Europhile project of transferring loyalties to the European Union, is wholly out of keeping with the trends of our time. For the creation and acceptance of the nation state worldwide is certainly one of the most striking – and potentially the most hopeful developments – of the past twentieth century.

The truth about the nation state is complex. It is Janus-faced: one side, the ugly chauvinistic half, associated with hostility to outsiders and intolerance of difference and the other, smiling side, the friend of liberty, the enemy of tyranny, colonialism and imperialism.

As we move into the new millennium, it is true that for the first time in recorded history the majority of mankind dwell within the political structure of the nation state; that is to say, in independent states, ruled by leaders who share their own culture and language. The great empires in which most of mankind was, over the centuries, forced to live are no more. The combination of defeat in war and internal struggle for self government has utterly destroyed them. The First World War brought to an end the old Ottoman, Habsburg and Tsarist empires in Europe and the Middle East. The Second World War and its aftermath have ended the French, the Dutch, the Belgian, the Portuguese and, largest of them all, the British empires. Finally, the end of the Cold War has brought the demise of the bogus Union States, the Union of Soviet Socialist Republic and of Yugoslavia. What were previously provinces and protectorates have joined those that were previously colonies in becoming independent, self-governing states. The doctrine of self-determination that Woodrow Wilson, the American President, preached to the victors and vanquished of the First World War is now – almost – universally accepted.

The magnitude and implications of this great change is seldom recognised. Yet it is one of – if not *the* most – dominant legacies left by the twentieth century. When the League of Nations was founded in 1919, after the defeat of Austria-Hungary, Turkey and the Russia of the Tsars, there were forty two founder members of that League; the largest single group was the sixteen separate states of Latin America, followed by fifteen European States, five Commonwealth countries and just six others. In 1945, when the successor body the United Nations was launched, it embraced only 54 states. But today, fifty six years later, the number totals 190. However enlightened the rule by others might be, and unless a shared history has produced an exceptionally successful merging of different traditions and cultures, the desire for self-rule and independence has become the imperative demand of the human race in all the continents of the globe.

To be ruled by those who are recognised as compatriots is far from a guarantee of good government – or successful government. But it has a legitimacy which even chaos, corruption and tyranny do not wholly undermine. The next great advance from, and often the companion of, self-government is democracy *within* the nation state. Since the end of the Cold War, in the past decade, virtually the whole of Latin America has moved from the rule of generals and presidents to that of elected governments and parliaments. Even in Russia, with no democratic tradition to invoke, universal free elections have been and are being held. Not only does democratic government make for better government and for more stable government but it greatly reduces the danger of that scourge of mankind: war. Democracies often wage war – but they seldom start them.

The 190 nations that exist today are of all shapes and sizes. In population, they range from the few hundred thousand who live in sovereign Kuwait and in the other thinly populated states of the Arabian Gulf to the giant 1,000 plus millions in China and India. In territory, they range from the few square miles of the Islands states of Cyprus, Fiji, the Maldives and elsewhere to the Continental spread of Canada, the United States, Australia and Russia. In prosperity, they stretch from the $170 and $260 income per head per annum of the people of Burundi and Bangladesh to the $28,020 per head of the United States, the $34,510 of the Norwegians, and the almost unbelievable annual per capita income of $44,350 dollars of the Swiss.

Their relationships with their geographical neighbours and with the world community generally are to all countries enormously important and the international rule of law has to be both extended and observed if an acceptable harmony is to be achieved.

But, outside Western Europe, there is not one of these 190 states, however recent in origin, however poor in income, however vulnerable to external attack, that wishes to abandon its independence and merge itself into the political structure of a more powerful neighbour, however well-disposed that neighbour may be.

Of course agreements and treaties between states are endlessly negotiated. Some are concerned with defence but by far the largest number are concerned with forging trading links with neighbour states in different parts of the world. So we have MERCOSUR, bringing together in South America, Argentina, Brazil, Paraguay, Uruguay – and soon Chile – in an evolving free trade area. In North America, NAFTA, joining Canada and Mexico with the United States, is now a well-established free trade area. Less developed is APEC, joining the great countries in the Pacific region, the United States, Japan and Australasia with China; and ASEAN, embracing Indonesia, Malaysia, Thailand and the Philippines. The Indian subcontinent has its own South Asian Co-operation Association, a still developing forum but one where at least some of the problems affecting India and its neighbours, Pakistan, Bangladesh, Nepal, and Sri Lanka, can be discussed.

But essentially these are trading organisations, dedicated to removing long-established trade barriers between countries and continents. They are *not* embryo states, with law-making powers that are binding upon their members.

Nor, as far as can be judged, have any of these groups the intention to go further. Canada lives, cheek by jowl, with its superpower neighbour the United States. Canada has its own currency, its own national bank, its own interest rates and monetary policy. It has every intention of retaining them.

In Latin America, in spite of the common culture that two centuries of Spanish rule imposed (with the solitary exception of Brazil) on the whole continent – the shared Catholic faith, the Spanish language – there is no discernible movement for merger and state formation.

Nor can any such movement be identified in the continents of Africa or Asia. Indeed the process of new nation formation may not yet have ended: and if so, it is more likely to reveal itself in China, India, Indonesia and Russia than anywhere else.

Only in Western Europe – and to a much lesser extent in the Eastern European applicant states dragged in behind – is the opposite process at work. Only here is the last desperate effort being made to ram together, in largely undemocratic institutions, the separate nations and states of Europe.

And why? As has already been documented in earlier chapters, the drive and momentum spring from the history of its two most powerful states, France and Germany, from their long struggle for hegemony; and within living memory from Nazi Germany's subjection and occupation of all its geographical neighbours. Since Germany's defeat in 1945, the effort of France, Italy and the three Benelux countries, has been to find new ways and a new political structure that would contain and control Germany so that never again would she dominate and conquer her European neighbours.

That is wholly understandable and in no way to be derided. But the UK was not defeated and occupied – even if, at times, some of our more demented Europhiles seem almost to regret it – and Britain has, with its distinctive and happier history, a different assessment of how its own future security and that of Europe can best be safeguarded.

4. Alternative Futures

There is one further point to be made. Where, in the long list of 190 sovereign, self-governing states stands the United Kingdom? Like many nations we are a modest people: we do not like the boastful and self-assertive and seldom wish to exaggerate our claims. But, in terms of economic strength, as measured by our Gross Domestic Product, we are the fifth or sixth largest in the world; in terms of military power, we are one of the five fully equipped nuclear powers and possess conventional forces (naval, air and ground) certainly in quality and effectiveness among the top half dozen; in terms of influence and diplomatic reach, with membership of the Commonwealth, the Anglo-American Alliance, NATO and the European Union and one of the five permanent veto-wielding members of the United Nations Security Council, we rank probably number three or four in the international pecking order. And beyond all that we possess two continuing assets that simply cannot be quantified: the growing ubiquity of our language and the creative potential of our people.

So, the Europhile claim that Britain is a weak and exhausted nation is patently false: and so is their claim that the British people cannot afford to make choices about their own future. The argument that it is now inevitable that we immerse ourselves ever-more deeply into the European Union, if need be becoming a province in the emerging European state, is not just misguided and based upon a flawed reading of the history of our times: it is an absurd notion.

The real problem for the United Kingdom is not lack of choice, but rather making that combination of choices which will be most beneficial to ourselves, to the different associations of which we are a member and to the causes for which we stand in the wider world.

5

Inside the European Union

New Options

The dream of Jean Monnet, the creation of the United States of Europe and the Franco-German reconciliation and integration project that has from the start underpinned it, have yet to be fully realised.

But how the integrationist cause has prospered. From the European Coal and Steel Community of 1952, through the Common Market and the Euratom Treaties of 1957, to the Single European Act of 1986, the Maastricht Treaty of 1992 and its successor at Amsterdam in 1997, the process of integration has maintained momentum and extended massively in scope and depth. And over these years, the Founding Six have been joined first by the UK, Eire and Denmark in 1973; then by Greece in 1981; followed by Spain and Portugal in 1986 and, most recently, by Sweden, Finland and Austria in 1996.

With the exceptions of Norway, Switzerland and Iceland, the nation states of Western Europe who came together in NATO to deter the perceived threat of Soviet aggression, along with the Cold War neutrals, Austria, Finland, Eire and Sweden are now members of the European Union – and governed by its institutions and subject to its laws, policies and commitments.

No one who has lived through these developments and witnessed the apparently unstoppable logic of Common Market leading to

Single Market – Single Market to single currency – Foreign Policy co-operation to the Common Foreign and Security Policy – from free movement of goods, labour and capital to a 'Europe without frontiers' will be easily persuaded that the process of integration has reached its end.

Self-evidently, it has not. Indeed the lines of advance are clearly mapped. Harmonisation of indirect taxes – corporation tax, custom duties and VAT – is an identified target with recent disputes over the withholding tax and codes of conduct to end allegedly unfair tax competition acting as advance guards or probes into still-defended national territory.

Still more important is the development of the Common Foreign Policy itself and the effort to establish a European Defence capability to give back-up to the European Union's external policy.

Britain's New Labour Europhiles, led by the Prime Minister, the Foreign Secretary and by both the former Defence Secretary and his successor, are particularly attracted to the Foreign Policy and Defence project where, with the war in Kosovo judged to have been a huge short-term success, they see the opportunity of placing Britain 'at the heart of Europe' – better still, of Britain leading Europe.

The third main sector for the advance of the European project is the strengthening of its supranational institutions. The December 1999 Heads of Government Council of Ministers meeting in Helsinki, formally launched the Inter-Governmental Conference that is to bring about, before enlargement, a more powerful and coherent Brussels Commission, an extended role for the European Parliament and a major extension of qualified majority voting, in place of the veto and the unanimity rule, in the Council of Ministers.

It would be surprising if the newly launched Inter-Governmental Conference did not embrace the other issue postponed at Amsterdam: namely, granting the European Union an explicit legal personality, to be recognised in international law. The *European*

Community, as distinct from the *European Union*, has of course long been recognised as an explicit legal entity, empowered to act as a sovereign institution in all matters to do with trade. The European Community was a member of GATT and is now of course a member of the World Trade Organisation (WTO). The member states of the European Union are also members of the WTO, but they can no longer speak, let alone negotiate, in that forum. The European Commission and its Commissioner for External Trade, speaks for them all. Similarly, in the G7 (now G8) – the informal group of major economic powers where representatives of Germany, France, Italy and the UK sit alongside representatives of the United States, Canada and Japan (and since 1996 Russia as well) – the European Community is now present, represented either by the Commission President or the Commissioner for External Affairs. In the World Bank and the IMF, the European nation states are still present. But, since they now have no currencies, it is the representative of the European Central Bank, along with the appropriate commissioner, who speaks for Germany, France and Italy.

What Amsterdam failed to achieve – and the opposition of both John Major and Tony Blair undoubtedly helped – was the recognition of the *European Union* as an explicit legal personality, with the international recognition and status that goes with it: in short, to accord it the same status, rights and privileges, as those long enjoyed by the *European Community*. To change that remains an important – if largely concealed – objective of the Europhiles. Although the Europhiles do not bruit it abroad just now, it is certain, sooner or later, to appear on the Heads of Government agenda. Indeed, the newly-appointed High Representative, Mr Solana, jumped the gun and, in support of an Italian proposal, stated his belief that the European Union should have not only international recognition but also a place on the United Nations Security Council, as a new permanent member. Whether the European Union representative would sit

128

alongside those of the UK and France and, if so, for how long, was not made clear. But it is certainly not far-fetched to envisage a steady build-up of first seconded, then directly recruited, European Union Foreign Office and Defence presence, with offices located no doubt alongside existing Commission Trade and Information staffs in all the capitals of the world. At first they would co-exist with existing Diplomatic Representatives of the fifteen Nation States but, in time, replace these increasingly redundant national diplomats. It certainly will be argued that this is the logical outcome of a Common Foreign Policy and the need to speak with one voice in support of it. And think of the savings this would bring to a modern Chancellor of the Exchequer: an almost irresistible temptation.

Hardly noticed, the most recent European Treaty, the Amsterdam Treaty, has given additional power and authority to the President of the European Commission – and to the European Parliament which relates, so parasitically, to him and his Commission. He is now formally vested with the duty of giving political leadership to that body, with the right to appoint and dismiss the individual commissioners in his Commission team.

These additional powers give extra significance to the appointment of Signor Romano Prodi as the new President in 1999, a strong and declared federalist whose first pronouncement – between his nomination for the post and its ratification – was on the need for the European Union to have, at its disposal, a European Army. And alongside the Commission President there now stands the High Representative, the former NATO Secretary General, Mr Solana who will increasingly speak for the fifteen foreign ministers to the world outside.

Of course the Europe that already exists and the still more integrated European Union of tomorrow face the UK and its people with the all too familiar dilemma. Are we ready to become truly and wholeheartedly European? To go with the tide? Or to grumble and resist? To be the odd man out, the brake on the forward momentum – in Prodi's words, the 'ball and chain' on European progress?

And if we want to be at the heart of Europe? Surely, we must go forward. Yet are we not pledged to retain the veto on tax matters, on a European Army and on institutional change, and is not our position with the British people that we are committed only to European co-operation and are resolutely opposed to the very idea – not of course that it has any serious sponsorship – of federal-type integration?

It is enough to produce a collective nervous breakdown in the Europhile political establishment of the UK. But they will, courageously, resolve it. We must choose. And the choice will be 'Yes' to Europe and to a new European future in the new Millennium, without all the clutter and detritus that a thousand years of history have deposited upon us.

That is the nightmare. But can we escape it? Can we say 'Yes' to what suits us and 'No' to what doesn't? Can we 'pick and choose' within our Membership of the European Community and our signature on the European treaties?

The conventional wisdom says that we can't. But the answer is in fact far less clear than many of the pundits proclaim. Indeed, it can be argued that we have done little else but opt-out since the day we joined. Certainly we have delayed. Following the 1975 Referendum the first main new European issue to come before Parliament was the proposal for direct elections to the European Parliament, the elections to be conducted on a broadly common basis, that is to say using the PR system generally in use on the Continent. In spite of the government's support, low-key admittedly, Parliament liked it so little and debates in the Commons were so prolonged that the date for direct elections was entirely missed. Afterwards, right down to the moment twenty years later when the New Labour government introduced, by resorting to the 1911 Parliament Act, its disgraceful closed regional list system – the system that denies the voter the right to vote for candidates of his choice but only for a list chosen by a Party committee – successive UK governments continued to conduct European Parliamentary elections on the traditional British, single constituency, first-past-the-post basis.

The second post-membership European initiative in 1979 was that of the Commission President, Roy Jenkins, to introduce the European Monetary System (EMS), with its main instrument, the Exchange Rate Mechanism (ERM) for fixing and adjusting exchange rates among member states and in relation to the new European currency, the Ecu. The British government, with James Callaghan as Prime Minister and Denis Healey as Chancellor, at once decided that the ERM was not for us – while agreeing to sign up to the virtually empty and declaratory EMS itself. As I already described, in spite of continuing pressures for UK membership of the ERM, it was not until 1990 that the then Prime Minister, Margaret Thatcher, reluctantly acceded to the pleas of her Chancellor John Major and brought sterling into the ERM – from which, barely two disastrous years later, it had to be peremptorily withdrawn amidst scenes of turmoil and crisis.

Then again at Maastricht, the most ambitious treaty since the founding Rome Treaty of 1957, the British largely opted out. The treaty itself bears the federalist print of the ablest of the Commission Presidents, Jacques Delors, together with the almost frantic resolve of Mitterand's France and Kohl's Germany to take European integration a giant further leap forward, following the collapse of the Berlin Wall and the reunion of East with West Germany .

Here indeed are precedents for a 'pick and choose' approach. If one wanted a model of a collective enterprise where one major partner gave general support but insisted on opt-outs for nearly all its concrete arrangements and measures, one would look not so much at Britain and Europe but at France and NATO. From the return of de Gaulle to power in 1958 until well beyond the end of the Cold War in the mid-1990s, France withdrew its forces from all the unified military commands, naval, and air, as well as ground, in NATO; expelled NATO forces and its HQ from French soil while retaining its seat and voice – and substantial influence – in NATO's Council Chamber.

But the development which gives the greatest credence to some lasting acceptance of a non-uniform, two-tier (or several tiered) Europe, is the current mammoth project of enlargement. With the end of the Cold War and the collapse of the (mainly) Soviet-imposed Communist regimes in Eastern Europe, the question of new members inevitably arose. But the scale and significance of what is involved have even now scarcely registered.

The treaties say little about who can join – except that membership is open, potentially to 'any European state' which applies. The single clause involved requires the applicant to enter into an agreement with the existing member states, an agreement that needs to be ratified by them all. An applicant also needs the assent of an absolute majority of the European Parliament. Custom and practice, as developed over more than four decades, demands of candidates democratic government, a broadly market economy and acceptance of the *acquis communautaire* – what has been already agreed and what has been pledged for the future, the ever-closer union. In the early 1990s, the years that immediately followed the collapse of Communism, the newly-liberated countries had to find their way. But all turned, with greater and lesser degrees of success, to forms of democratic government, to the abandonment of central planning and to the large-scale privatisation of formerly state industries. Between April 1994 and June 1996 no less than ten states applied. Of these, the Council judged that Poland, the Czech Republic, Hungary, Slovenia, Estonia and Cyprus should be given priority and instructed the Commission to examine and report back on the capacity of those applicant states to meet the requirements of membership.

Negotiations began in March 1998. If successful, membership of the European Union would increase from its existing fifteen to twenty one – the largest single increase in membership since the EC was created. Recognising the magnitude of the changes involved, both for the existing members and the applicants, the Commission, sensibly, was required to report on the general impact of extending membership to the six. Its report, Agenda 2000, analysed the problems involved and the magnitude of the changes required both of applicants and member states.

Then, in a dramatic move, the implications of which have yet to be stated, let alone seriously addressed – inspired largely by the desire to reward Romania and Bulgaria for their help in the Kosovo war as well as by widespread anxieties about the stability of the fledgling new democracies in former communist countries – the Helsinki Heads of Government Council of Ministers in December 1999 agreed that the negotiations for enlargement should now embrace, not just the named six but a further five applicants and, for good measure, Turkey as well.

Here is a project of immense scope and complexity that dwarfs all those previously encountered. The problems involved can be most simply described by looking first at those that the applicant states have to surmount and then those large accommodations and changes that the existing members will have to undertake.

Historically, economic progress and success have featured much more strongly in Western and Central Europe than in the East. The War, the half century of Communist-imposed rule that followed it, added to this already long-established divergence between the two halves of the Continent. While Eastern Europe was largely restricted in trade and development to serving the needs of the Soviet Union, Western Europe and Germany enjoyed first the great beneficence of the Marshall Plan and then the opening up, within Europe and worldwide, of trade and capital investment.

The resulting gap in competitiveness and efficiency between Eastern Europe and the European Union is the first of the problems that the East has to confront. Eastern Europe has of course the advantage of cheap labour and much lower employment-related social costs. More, it has substantial numbers of skilled workers and professional people. But – to take only the largest of the applicant countries Poland – there is a clear risk that its heavily manned steel industry and its famous Gdansk shipyards will not survive unrestrained competition with the steel and shipbuilding industries of the European Union.

Joining the European Union has become steadily more difficult over the decades. I remember well the volumes of European legislation, the directives, regulations, decisions and treaties which we in Britain simply had to swallow whole when we joined the European Community in 1973. Today, in depth and scope, the legislation and treaties that make up the *acquis communautaire* fill not so much a bookshelf as a library. And among them lie all those obligations to raise environmental standards, to improve health and safety, to end discrimination between men and women, to limit the working week which inevitably add heavy costs to the already uncompetitive East. In Poland again it has been authoritatively estimated that no less than 3 per cent of its GDP would need to be spent for at least a decade to implement the environmental requirements of the European Union.

On top of all this there are of course the almost unchecked power of the Commission to veto what it regards as a state aid, direct or indirect, and the fact that state aids are still an important contributor to the economies and industries of Eastern Europe.

Still more important – and potentially crippling – to the economies of Eastern Europe would be the obligation to join a single currency, the euro, and to accept all that is required of them through membership of the Economic and Monetary Union. This has been partially recognised in the negotiations. Applicant countries are not required to actually join the single currency at the time of entry. But they have to accept the commitment and they have to adhere to the aims of Economic and Monetary Union.

To complete the picture, applicant countries must also observe the so-called Copenhagen criteria. These require not just the institutions of democracy but guarantees of the rule of law, human rights and protection of minorities, and, apart from a functioning market economy, their open-ended commitment to Political, Economic and Monetary Union.

A formidable task indeed, but one that the applicant states have little option but to undertake. Yet, when one turns to what is required of the existing member states, it may well seem that theirs is the heavier burden.

First of course is the problem of the Common Agricultural Policy (CAP). Defended from more efficient external producers by its system of variable levies, which make it literally impossible for low cost foreign producers to undercut domestic farmers, and with its system of buying without quantitative limit the main home-grown foodstuffs at a high guaranteed price, and then taking surpluses either into intervention and buying in huge warehouse stores and refrigeration plants, or exporting to other countries at subsidised prices, it is inevitably a costly arrangement. Moreover it is one that has bestowed great prosperity on the farmers of France and Germany, Holland and Denmark and on the citrus-growing and olive oil producers of the Mediterranean – Italy, Spain and Greece. In spite of widespread and continuing demands for its reform, the CAP remains substantially intact and still absorbs just under 50 per cent of the total Community budget. Without massive change – or huge increase in costs – it cannot be extended to the applicant countries of Eastern Europe, themselves overwhelmingly agricultural countries producing and selling their products at prices far below those prevailing in the European Union. The European Commission, in its Agenda 2000

Report, which was penned to address the problems of enlargement for the six applicants of 1997, did manage to produce a far from convincing plan for the years 2000 to 2006 that combined gradual change in the CAP of the fifteen with preparatory pre-entry expenditures to assist the six new applicants.

But whatever credibility Agenda 2000 had was lost in the Berlin Heads of Government Summit in March 1999 when President Chirac virtually tore it up – in favour of the near status quo and the French farmer. So what has now emerged – although governments including our own are very coy about admitting it – is a new demand on the applicant states: that they should accept all the conditions of membership but that they themselves should not be included in the guaranteed price provisions of the CAP. Even the most supplicant applicants do not conceal their rage.

The CAP is only part of the change required in the existing policies of the European Union. Most of the remaining non-CAP expenditure of the Community Budget is taken up with the structural funds. These include the funding of regional policy, job training and the so-called Cohesion Fund – the special grant made to the colloquially called 'poor four', of Spain, Portugal Greece and Ireland whose per capita income was significantly below the EU average in return for their agreement to join the single currency. This has made a large and very welcome contribution to the economies and living standards of the countries and people involved. But there can be no question that, once enlargement begins, the claims of the present 'poor four' and of the existing assisted regions will be totally outstripped by those of the East European entrants. Today the most prosperous applicant state, the Czech Republic, enjoys only 60 per cent of the EU average per capita income, while Hungary and Poland achieve only 49 and 39 per cent respectively of the EU average living standards.

Clearly, if the applicant states are to meet the requirements of membership, they will need financial assistance from the existing members. In their Agenda 2000 document, the Commission acknowledges the need and makes some financial provision up to the year 2006. But again, it is hopelessly unrealistic, for the whole financial exercise is done within the current level of Community taxation where total revenues are fixed by treaty not to exceed 1.27 per cent of total Community Gross Domestic Product. And underlying this dubious arithmetic is an assumed rate of growth in the European Union of 2.5 per cent per annum in the six year period ahead.

It is now clear that the figures do not add up. The European Union growth rate is unlikely to achieve the 2.5 per cent level; the CAP, post-Berlin, is far more costly than the original estimates assumed; the number of applicant states is not six but at least twelve – yet there has been no recognition of the new facts either by the Commission, our own government or by the governments of our European neighbours.

The obvious remedy is a substantial increase in the European Union's tax revenues, the so-called 'own resources' of the European Union, an increase that would take those revenues well above the 1.27 per cent figure that now obtains. On the face of it, even if it was to rise to 2.27 per cent sensible people would not say 'impossible' – although raising the money would go against the low taxation doctrine embedded in the Maastricht Treaty and the tax-cutting policies of most of the member states. But that leaves out the very important fact that the composition of the 'own resources' taxes and in particular the very unequal burden that they impose upon the member states are subjects of explosive sensitivity. Mrs Thatcher's relentless four-year campaign to reduce the disproportionate initial British contribution is sufficient testimony to that. And there is the certain knowledge that any increase in this tax ceiling or even any extension of the present position which is due for review and amendment by 2002, will produce fierce disputes among the existing fifteen member states in which the reduction of the UK's rebate will be, for many of them, a major target.

And there is one further problem to be faced: a problem difficult in itself, but in the prevailing political correctness of the European Union so challenging to its most basic claims that it is hardly ever mentioned, let alone confronted: the problem of free movement of labour.

It is here of course that that immense gap, already noted, between the living standards of the average citizens of the existing and the applicant countries becomes so potent. Men and women virtually everywhere, other things being equal, prefer to live their lives in the communities in which they are born, grow up, work, marry and make their homes. But other things are not always equal. And if poverty, unemployment, lack of opportunity for one's children are virtually inescapable in one's community of origin, then for most people the natural solution is, however painful, to pull up one's roots and move to where the opportunities for finding work and for enjoying a better life are greater. In our own country, in spite of enormously costly and long-sustained regional policies to help create work in what used to be called the Development Areas – mainly, Scotland, Wales, the North, North West and the South West – the movement of people into the prosperous, job-plentiful areas of London, the South, the East Midlands and East Anglia has continued apace these past fifty years. Of course, in the case of the UK – apart from the continuing flow of British people to the countries of the English-speaking world – the search for work and greater opportunities can normally be satisfied within the territory of our own country.

But this will not be the case – or only to a very limited extent – in Eastern Europe. Vast numbers of unemployed and underemployed can be expected to move into the well favoured prosperous areas of the European Union. True, there is at present substantial unemployment in France, Germany and Italy too. But the migrant army of willing workers will be ready, as migrant labour always is, to accept less pay and poorer working conditions. And, if work is at first only intermittent, the unemployment pay and Social Security Benefits are, compared to those available in their own countries, almost unbelievably generous.

Already – and indeed for some years past – the hungry and the hopeful in growing numbers press upon the porous frontiers of the European Union; and it isn't just the mobile workers of Eastern Europe but growing numbers from Russia and the former States of the Soviet Union, from the Middle East and elsewhere who seek entry.

The European Union is indeed conscious of the need for creating its own external frontiers, with a Europe-wide immigration and asylum policy, backed up with effectively policed borders and accelerated administrative and judicial processes.

But Eastern Europe, the Europe of the applicant countries, will not be *outside*: it will be *inside* the European Union. Within that 'Europe without frontiers' – that much-loved entity of the nation-hating Europhiles. Are they now to discriminate? To apply quantitative limits to the inflow? And what decisions do they expect, given the words of the treaties, from the European Court of Justice when those cases come before it?

Of course, people of one nation, one language and one culture can absorb, and benefit from the settlement in their midst of people from very different backgrounds and cultures. But no one can doubt the process of absorption and adjustment is immensely helped if the newcomers share some significant experience or connection with the host country.

And still more the process is eased if the authorities make additional social and community provisions to cope with the inevitable increase in pressure upon local facilities and if the influx takes place at a measured pace. The UK's own experience can again be cited. The post-war years have brought, in substantial numbers, new communities to live among us. In some areas, relations have been tense and hostile: but few will doubt that the process has been greatly eased by the common linguistic heritage that former British rule left in the West Indies and in much of the Indian subcontinent. Similarly, although not without difficulty, France has taken into itself large numbers of people from North Africa, and in particular Algeria, previously under French rule.

To put the problem as undramatically as possible: a large number of people from the new member states of Eastern Europe can be reasonably expected to present themselves in the most prosperous areas of the European Union. The flow might be reduced if a very strong and expensive regional and 'poor four' type of policy was introduced to help create work in the new member states. Similarly, the problem of absorption in the host areas will be eased if substantial funds were made available by the governments concerned to reduce the pressure on accommodation and community services.

Such measures however cannot be relied upon. And even if pursued, large problems would still remain. Their solution will not be helped by the fact that public opinion in the existing member states, while still almost totally uninformed about the difficulties that lie ahead, is far from enthusiastic about enlargement. On average 42 per cent are in support. While the UK at 40 per cent is close to the average, the two most influential and certainly affected players, Germany and France, record only 38 and 33 per cent respectively.

So what is to be done? One obvious response is to negotiate with the applicant states long – and for some very long – transitional periods before they have to accept all the rigours of membership – and before they can obtain all the rights that go with it. The 'transitional period' is indeed a time-honoured device in European construction.

But on this occasion the Europhiles are, understandably, hesitant.

5. *Inside the European Union*

As a recent report of the very Euro-friendly House of Lords European Select Committee concluded:

> Member States must come to grips with the fact that the price of accelerated enlargement may well be the acceptance of what would amount to a two-tier European Union Membership for several years to come.

(Two-tier, that dreaded Eurosceptic word.) The Government in its response to the Select Committee was swift to assert:

> The acceptance of limited transition periods does not imply a two-tier Europe.

But, as our own and other governments will, sooner or later, be forced to acknowledge, it almost certainly does. And this lesson is likely to be learnt during this year of grace 2000, the year by whose end the European Heads of Government have pledged themselves to reach conclusions and to take decisions on the changes required by the institutions of the European Union to accommodate enlargement; the IGC launched by the European Council in Helsinki in December 1999 is to report back by the end of the year 2000.

With President Prodi in the lead, with the strong encouragement of the September 1999 Report of the Three Wise Men – former Belgian Prime Minister Dehaene, recently retired German President Weizsäcker and our own Lord Simon, former Minister for European Trade, now personal advisor to the Prime Minister – and with the agreement of all fifteen heads of government that a Europe of twenty seven would be ungovernable with institutions designed to meet the needs of the Founding Six, there is a strong likelihood that they will learn this lesson too. Moreover with an agenda for change already long debated – and nearly agreed – in the negotiations that led up to

141

the 1997 Amsterdam Treaty, there will be exceptional pressures to reach agreement at least on limiting the number of commissioners and on reducing to a minimum in the Council of Ministers existing veto rights.

At present each of the four largest member states (Germany, France, Italy and the UK) have the right to nominate two commissioners while all other states have the right each to nominate one. As membership of the Union has grown, the College of Commissioners has grown with it – and there are now barely enough significant portfolios to go around. Add another twelve and the situation would indeed be absurd. So, the number has to be reduced: and the obvious first target is for the Big Four each to renounce their second commissioner.

But that will not be enough. The rule of one member/one commissioner will have to be changed and some form of election will have to take its place.

The other, still more important change will be to the voting system on the Council of Ministers. At present, the big four each have 10 votes, Spain has 8, Greece, Portugal, Belgium and The Netherlands each have 5, Sweden and Austria 4, Finland, Ireland and Denmark 3 – and Luxembourg 2. A total of 62 is the qualified majority necessary for making decisions. Put the other way round, a blocking minority must total 24. In certain very important areas of the treaty – in number much reduced – the requirement for unanimity remains in the Council of Ministers: the veto.

The favoured trade-off that emerged during the Amsterdam negotiations was the further restriction of the right of veto and in exchange, taking more account of different population size, GDP and other factors, a reweighting of the votes better to reflect the obvious differences of scale between them.

On the face of it this is a common-sense move. The obvious absurdity is for Luxembourg, with a population of 0.1 per cent of its German neighbour, to possess 2 votes in the Council of Ministers that accords Germany only 10. And perhaps the ultimate absurdity is that Luxembourg, like all the other member states, however small, possesses the veto on such crucial matters as tax harmonisation and the admission of new members. Once admitted, the same veto rights would be available to the East European applicants and to the two Island States, Malta and Cyprus, with their very small populations.

With such compelling facts, agreement on change might appear to be both desirable and inevitable. Only the British, it would be alleged, with their stubborn and public commitment to maintain its veto on tax matters and on all other matters that affect our vital interests, appear to be a significant obstacle.

Within the context of the IGC, and if it remains narrowly focused on the constitutional-institutional matters referred to, then it may be that, not for the first time, the UK will find itself in a minority of one.

But, that is by no means certain. It could be, in the event, very different indeed. One has only to consider the list of applicant states, the great gulf in historical experience that separates them from the countries of Western Europe, and in particular from the Founding Six, to realise that, even with the almost crazed ambition of Commissioner Prodi to create a United Europe, the old dream of a French-led, Franco-German hegemony in a European State can no longer be achieved. The divisions and diversities of Prodi's Europe are simply too large for the Europe of the Six to manage, to integrate and to absorb.

The frontiers of the applicant twelve already lie one thousand miles beyond the borders of Charlemagne's empire. Nor is that the ultimate end. Within the decade, there will be still more countries knocking on the doors of the European Union. With Slovenia as one of the twelve, for how long can the rest of former Yugoslavia be excluded? – the mini-states of Croatia, Bosnia, Macedonia, perhaps Montenegro, perhaps Kosovo as well as Serbia itself and neighbouring Albania? And with the Baltic States, Estonia, Latvia and

Lithuania within the European Union, why should not the Ukraine, Belarus, and Moldavia, if they wish, be candidates for membership?

Perhaps wisely – perhaps not – no one has yet attempted to define Europe in geographical terms. Certainly, the only recent reference to the limits of Europe is to be found in the Presidency conclusions, issued at the end of the Cologne European Council Meeting on 4 June 1999. In anticipating a meeting between the European Union and the three Transcaucasion Presidents, the Presidency conclusions refer to *'the importance of the Transcaucasus for stability at the dividing line between Europe and Asia'*. The inference is clear, that Armenia, Azerbaijan and Georgia are European States at the frontier where Europe and Asia meet – and must therefore be, in principle, eligible for membership. Indeed the question arises: what is Europe and where exactly does Europe end? With Turkey added to the officially-recognised applicant list at the subsequent Helsinki Council meeting, the question does need an answer. But, as it stands, it could well be that up to a further dozen applicants will have to be considered within the next decade.

It is of course conceivable that the newly united Germany, with its government again centred in Berlin and with the greater self-confidence of a new political generation in power, largely free from the guilt of Nazi tyranny and Nazi aggression, could see in this great tilt to the East opportunities not only for expanding trade and accelerating economic growth but for playing a far greater role in the politics of the whole European Union and a dominant position for itself in its relations with the East. But it is difficult to see how this could be reconciled with the basic post-war commitment to partnership with France – and it is nearly impossible to envisage French governments willingly abandoning their whole post-war strategy for the revival of France based on partnership with Germany and on maximising their power through the institutions of the European Union.

5. Inside the European Union

Whatever the future of the Franco-German relationship, the inescapable fact is that the Europe of fifteen is almost certain to become a Europe of twenty seven or twenty eight within this decade and with the prospect of a further ten applicants in the period further ahead.

This brings us back to the whole question of a two-tier or indeed a multi-tier Europe. France, unless Germany breaks the deep links that have been forged, will not willingly accept the dilution that such a Europe will impose. It can be fudged – indeed for several years – by the device of the prolonged transition period. But sooner or later it is bound to bring in to the decision-making institutions those countries with interests and connections very different from her own.

Here, surely, is the great opportunity for British diplomacy. Enlargement on the scale that is now envisaged poses the greatest dilemma that the Union has faced. To go ahead with the enlargement project means the abandonment of the strategic aim, that 'ever-closer union' that the Six set for themselves and which has given such momentum over the decades, and its replacement by a much looser association. Integration on the model of the Six is by no means the universal wish of the present applicant nations. They want membership with the international respectability and protection that goes with it and, above all, help in solving their massive economic problems.

If the UK plays its cards well, it will certainly not be alone in pressing for a long-term, probably permanent two-tier or multi-tier Europe, rather than a temporary one. Many member states are already half-convinced that this is now the most satisfactory option – indeed the only realistic option available.

The UK's argument can go further than that. We should remind ourselves and our Continental friends that the 1997 Treaty of Amsterdam – while avoiding the dread words 'two tier' – in fact specifically envisages and embodies it in treaty terms. In the so-called 'flexibility' clauses added to the Maastricht Treaty, Amsterdam introduces and defines the concept of 'closer co-operation' – a novel provision which permits the majority of member states, with the agreement of all, to introduce new integrationist policies and to use the institutions and procedures of the treaties, to help carry them out. There is no suggestion in the relevant Articles 11, 40, 43 and 44 which apply to the main European Community part of the treaties and to the so-called third pillar, dealing with Home Affairs and Justice, that the minority of member states who do not wish to join the majority in 'closer co-operation' should be in any way time limited in their abstention; or that, sooner or later, they should join up with the main body. What the clauses do allow for the non-joiners is, first, the right to veto 'closer co-operation', second, to be assured that 'closer co-operation' for the majority does not 'affect the competencies, rights, obligations and interests of those Member States which do not participate therein', nor 'constitutes a discrimination or a restriction of trade between Member States'. And last, that those who opt-out from 'closer co-operation' have the right, should they so wish, to subsequently join with the majority in the 'closer co-operation' arrangements and policies that they have developed.

Here indeed, and at long last, is that recognition in the treaties themselves that while the nation states of Europe can accept common rules and policies governing a substantial part of their affairs, diversity and difference must be accepted, not crushed and disciplined by the imposition of a single set of laws, policies and institutions covering the whole of their affairs.

This two-tiered Europe not only suits the United Kingdom and would permit, without inconceivable disruption, second-tier membership for most of the East European applicants, but it would allow France and Germany and their partners in the original six, plus a number of later adherents, to go ahead with their neo-federal or federal project, that 'ever-closer union', destined to end in the creation of a single state, the United States of Europe. To take, for illustrative purposes, one item already on the agenda: tax harmonisation. It is difficult to see any objection to France, Germany and indeed the other twelve member states, if they maintain their belief in the advantages of a large measure of tax harmonisation, from using Article 11 to bring this about. More, they could – and France and Germany with their long-established Eurocorps undoubtedly wish it – continue to develop collective armed forces to help carry out, in Europe, what they themselves and the Security Council of the United Nations believe to be necessary peacekeeping and peace-enforcing tasks. No one who has any memory of European history will fail to recall the tremendous effort that France made between 1950 and 1953 to create a European Defence Community, embracing the armed forces of Germany in the Six down to battalion level, under a common command – an effort finally and paradoxically aborted by the French Assembly itself. That project lingers on and it has been partially revived in recent years by the governments of both France and Germany not only in setting up the Eurocorps but in co-operation in defence procurement, including the merger of major defence equipment firms.

'Closer co-operation' in a two-tier Europe has in fact obvious attractions for both France and Germany – and their federalist allies. Some of the very real difficulties that face them and the existing European Union with the present enlargement proposals could thus be avoided.

And there is one additional matter, of sufficient importance to threaten the whole enlargement enterprise that must now be considered. The Franco-German thrust for a European defence community, which the Treaties of Maastricht and Amsterdam now formally embrace and which was powerfully reinforced by the UK in its still euphoric, post-Kosovo mood, is now committed to absorb and merge the defence arrangements of the long-established Western European

Union with the structures of the European Union. In short, the European Union is about to become a military alliance, and the obligations in the defence and foreign policy field, no less than in the economy, trade and environment areas, will fall upon the applicant states.

All the applicant East European States are former satellites of the USSR. A number of them share a common frontier with existing Russia. Some – the Baltic states of Estonia, Latvia and Lithuania – are former republics of the old Soviet Union – and so of course are a number of other former, not yet applicant, Soviet states now part of the Commonwealth of Independent States. Russian policy has always – and confusingly – been driven by a mixture of paranoia about expansionist neighbours and her fear of hostile encirclement, and her own great-power bullying of her neighbours to build buffer zones and to establish her own spheres of interest. But to bring the frontiers of a large armed quasi-state, the European Union, with Germany at its centre, to the very borders of Russia would indeed be a dangerous and to the Russians an unacceptable development.

It can be argued that the inclusion of Poland, Hungary and the Czech Republic in NATO, a few years ago, was itself an extremely risky enterprise – but one which then President Yeltsin's Russia had to accept. Encouraged by this, some in NATO are planning a further expansion to the East. Others, including the United States government and its Defence Department take a more cautious and restricted view of such a development. Poland and the Czech Republic, with their long history of partition and imperial subjection, have had as well an almost unique place in twentieth-century European history – as the victims of Nazi aggression, Soviet occupation and imposed Communist tyranny. That they should seek the protection from both their historical persecutors in membership of NATO is understandable – just – even in the Kremlin. The extension to Bulgaria and Rumania would be a more serious but not impossible risk. But for the

European Union, with its newly-agreed defence role, its absorption of the WEU, its development of its own separate, autonomous military capability and its continuing claim on NATO assets as well, to extend its geographical and political presence to incorporate the Baltic states, and later the Ukraine, Belarus, Moldavia and others with a common frontier with Russia, would be to take a gamble of huge dimensions. The visit of President Prodi to Latvia on 10 February 2000 and his statement there that 'any attack or aggression against a European Union member nation would be an attack or aggression against the whole EU, this is the highest guarantee' was not merely untrue but dangerous and irresponsible – and a vivid example of the presumption and worse of our would-be masters in Brussels.

Russia is – and will remain for some time ahead – a crippled, humiliated, paranoid giant but one that still possesses a vast decaying nuclear arsenal and substantial conventional forces as well. It is a vital interest of the West that Russia should be helped to achieve stability, democracy and prosperity. It is not entitled to a ring of satellite states, but it has a reasonable expectation that its old adversaries will see to it that it will be bordered by those who are at least militarily unaligned. It makes sense therefore that the Baltic and any East European applicant states, certainly those bordering Russia, should not be required – should not be allowed – to join the new military structures of the European Union. That is one more compelling argument for a two-tier or multi-tier Europe.

The whole concept of a two-tier Europe needs, urgently, intense study and exploration and the launch of a serious public debate in both Britain and Europe. The East European applicants can hardly be expected to take the lead, or to play more than a very minor role, for fear of adverse reactions in Brussels, and for fear of jeopardising or delaying membership. But for Britain, the advantage of early discussion, debate and preparation is obvious. Among other things, it would be a very reasonable expectation that – once they had recovered from the minor initial shock – our relations with most of our European neighbours would improve rather then deteriorate. In a European Union where the climate of opinion is powerfully against difference and dissent, minorities are at best a nuisance, an obstacle to the realisation of a great historical project. To play, almost permanently, the role of the odd man out, as the UK has done reluctantly, weakly, but yet repeatedly over its years of membership, is to invite opprobrium and censure. To the Europhiles and supporters of 'ever-closer union', Signor Prodi may have been a little undiplomatic but, essentially, they think he was right to describe the UK as the 'ball and chain' on the European advance.

Ironically, indeed maddeningly, the labels of narrow nationalism and anti-Europeanism have come to be attached to the one nation, the United Kingdom, that has, within living memory, and again and again in its history, successfully withstood some all-conquering European tyranny – has 'saved itself by its own exertions and Europe by its example' to quote William Pitt. Whatever the wishes of the majority of our political class may be, there is a strong opposite pull from the majority of the electorate: a pull not strong or hostile enough to demand or wish for total withdrawal but one that is only content with 'this far and no further' plus 'let's get rid of such self-evident nonsense as the CAP and the Common Fisheries Policy'. Some would go much further, others would not wish to go so far, but the great majority of our people are very near to the one slogan and one position that the present leader of the Conservative Party, William Hague, has successfully devised: 'In Europe but not run by Europe'.

It is this knowledge of the constraints that our own electorate places upon them, that forces the wretched Ministers of one government after another, in ever more frequent meetings of their appropriate European Councils – which themselves stretch evermore widely over nearly the whole field of political action – to play a kind of charade. In Brussels, helped by the ever-diligent highly knowledgeable army of UK officials stationed there, they seek to show goodwill and offer costless concessions and at the same time withhold consent to those proposals which really matter to most of our Council colleagues. Back home, they must trumpet successful resistance to Euro-pressures and then inform the Commons and the Lords that their ambition – unlike that of their predecessors – is to be at the heart of Europe while retaining, come what may, the veto in defence of our vital national interest. I understand it, but its fundamental falseness is disgusting.

Our European colleagues have passed through successive periods of interest, bewilderment and dismay. Dislike and contempt, not for Britain itself or its people, but for the posturing of British politicians has begun to emerge.

How different it will be when an open and honest British leadership, with the backing of its Parliament and people, states:

We can go no further. But we are your friend and most reliable ally and we wish you well in your further endeavours to deepen your integration and to create whatever form of state structure that bests meets your requirement and the wishes of your people.

We would expect no less happy and fruitful a relationship between our 58 million people and the 275 million people who have joined your political family, than now exists between the 25 million people of Canada and their great 250 million neighbour, the United States of America to the south.

Furious and anguished voices – mainly Europhile – will be heard, protesting against this eminently sensible prospect. And we shall be told that we shall be punished and penalised for our audacity. In particular we shall hear mouthings about 3 million British jobs that are linked with exports to the European Union markets. Joining this chorus, and not without prompting by influential UK Europhile politicians, will be the Chairmen and Managing Directors of large foreign firms who will assert that their investment in Sunderland, Swindon, Swansea or wherever is now at risk. Certainly they will be heard to mutter gloomily that the planned expansion project will have to be dropped and the Board is now considering the option of relocating its whole European subsidiary elsewhere on the Continent. So still more British jobs will purportedly be at risk.

It won't wash. Common sense alone blows away the threat of trade sanctions. If 3 million jobs are involved in British exports to Europe, then 3.25 million European Union jobs depend on free access to the UK market. A sobering thought.

But that apart, we all live – certainly all the advanced trading nations including the great economies of North America and Japan as well as the European Union itself – in a world trading system under treaties regulated by international law. Any attempt by the European Union to discriminate against the UK would be directly in breach of the main provisions of the World Trade Organisation. Condemnation and then authorisation of penal countermeasures by the UK would certainly be sanctioned by that body.

But this scenario is plainly fantasy. It would scarcely be plausible even if the EU was a hostile power – which it is not.

Certainly, foreign-owned firms would be concerned if the European Market was closed to their export sales. But that will not happen. There *could* be benefit from trading in Europe in a single currency, but that is far from certain and its weight among the investment factors involved is very small. Language, business culture, skilled and adaptable labour, access to capital, corporation tax rates, a competitive exchange rate (even, for some, a choice of golf courses) weigh far more heavily with corporate managers. While the threat to inward investment is small, there is of course a serious short-term problem for many exporters whose price-competitiveness has been undermined by the undervalued Euro. That does need corrective action by the Chancellor and the Bank of England, above all to lower UK short-term interest rates and thus discourage the inflow of speculative money which is pushing up the value of the pound.

To conclude, there is a possible future for Britain – and one that must have very considerable appeal to our EU partners – in a two-tier or multi-tier Europe – a tiered construct that is in any case demanded by the EU's new commitment to a vast enlargement to the East.

If there are obstacles and difficulties not faced in what has already been written and which require, with mutual benefit, a more limited treaty association than our membership of the European Community and European Union treaties involve, then there is an existing alternative which could be a model for that purpose: the European Economic Zone Treaty, which now includes a number of former EFTA – European Free Trade Area – states, most notably Norway, Switzerland and Iceland. The EEZ is basically a free trade area with non-tariff, open-trade arrangements with the European Union.

To those who think that a trade treaty in itself is bound to be far less satisfactory than a more embracing treaty of Community or Union, two points may be worth making. First, Switzerland and Norway are the richest per capita GDP states in the continent of Europe, second, no less than 59.7 per cent of Norway's exports and 56.4 per cent of Switzerland's are freely traded into the European Union.

There is indeed plenty of scope for Britain in Europe. But only if there is sufficient 'flexibility' on both sides.

6

The World Outside I

Britain and the Commonwealth

On 22 December 1999, the Presidents of Portugal and of the People's Republic of China stood side by side in Macao, as the Portuguese flag was lowered there for the last time. Thus was turned the last page of the last chapter in the long story of European Colonial rule.

It was a story that began nearly five hundred years before with the great maritime discoveries of Christopher Columbus, reaching the new world of the Americas in the name of Spain in 1492, and of Portugal's Vasco da Gama in 1494 sailing down the African coast to the Cape of Good Hope and then on, across the Indian Ocean, to the Asian Islands and mainland that lay far beyond to the East.

The discoveries of Spain and Portugal, the trading posts, the settlements and the conquests that ensued were soon emulated by the other European Atlantic-facing maritime powers: France, The Netherlands and England. After a century and a half of conquest and settlement, trade rivalry and war, the end of the Seven Years War in 1763 saw the emergence of England as the dominant Imperial power in North America, and in India as well. Portugal and Spain divided up between them virtually the whole of South America, while Spain, Holland, France and England acquired the many island territories of the West Indies and the Caribbean.

In Asia and the Pacific, the Dutch dominated the vast archipelago of the East Indies, Spain the Philippines while Portugal established trading stations in East Timor, in Goa in India and Macao in China. The Spanish, the Portuguese, the Dutch, the French and the English all had trading posts, settlements and conquered territories in various parts of Africa.

The end of the eighteenth century and the beginning of the nineteenth brought the American War of Independence, the French Revolution, the conquests and ultimate defeat of Napoleon – but not before Spain and Portugal, occupied by French troops, found their grip on their overseas territories much weakened.

The nineteenth century saw the end of direct Spanish rule in South America, and a process of independence and state formation that followed it. This was enormously encouraged by the 'hands off the Americas' policy, the Monroe doctrine, of the United States and by the virtual command of the seas by the British navy. Britain retained, despite American Independence, the vast territory of Canada, while in the Pacific Captain Cook opened the way for exclusive British rule in the vast and lightly populated continent of Australia, the islands of New Zealand and numerous other Pacific Island territories.

The nineteenth century saw, too, a renewed scramble for colonies and territories, centred mainly in Africa where latecomers Belgium, Germany and Italy joined the already strongly established British, French and Portuguese in the scramble to divide up what territories were still left outside direct European colonial rule.

The twentieth century, particularly its second half, has seen the progressive collapse of European colonialism. In virtually all colonial territories, movements demanding self-government arose and some were strong enough to wrest power from unwilling imperial rulers. But colonial independence movements were massively aided and reinforced by Nazi Germany's initial victories during the Second World War. With the defeat and occupation of Holland, Belgium and France in 1940, colonial rule was inevitably weakened in their overseas territories. In North Africa, while both Vichy France and its free

French successor, managed to maintain French control in both Morocco and Algeria, Tunisia was wholly in German hands and was the scene of the last battle in the long North Africa campaign when German forces were finally driven from the continent. The process was again reinforced by the initial victories of Japan, after December 1941, when Japanese troops occupied the Dutch East Indies, French Indo-China, including Vietnam, Cambodia and Laos, and the British territories of Hong Kong, Malaysia and Burma.

Following the defeat of the Axis powers in 1945, with the United States actively anti-colonialist, but with the limited help of British arms, attempts were made to restore the Dutch in Jakarta and the French in Hanoi, and Britain's own rule in Malaysia and Hong Kong.

But the returning Dutch were bitterly and strongly resisted. They soon abandoned the attempt to restore their rule in the East Indies and accepted the establishment of the new independent state of Indonesia. France returned to Indo-China and found itself engaged in a war of national liberation, led by the Communist Vietcong. After nearly a decade of fierce and costly struggle, and the great French defeat at Dien Bien Phu, France withdrew from the whole area. France was to meet the same problem in its North African territories a few years later. Arab nationalism, triumphant in Nasser's Egypt and in much of the Middle East, aroused and fed the demand for independence in Tunisia, Morocco and, most seriously, Algeria – an area of large French settlement, proclaimed by France to be a *'département'* of France itself. There again the forces of nationalism after years of bitter warfare proved to be too strong to be contained and it needed the return to power of General de Gaulle to handle and disguise the extent of the defeat and to accept the new independent state of Algeria.

Italy of course had lost its very recently acquired empire in Ethiopia and Libya, along with its longer held territories in Somalia and Eritrea to the advancing British forces in 1940-1. Belgium had retained the Congo in a state of fragile unity and without serious challenge to its rule – in spite of the occupation of its own territory – throughout the war and early post-war years. A sudden upsurge of African nationalism in 1961 led to a flight from empire that was, to put it gently, precipitate and damaging. Holland, as we have seen, had been pushed out of Indonesia, France from Indo-China while Germany had lost her African colonies at the end of the First World War – handed over to British and South African rule in League of Nations Mandate agreements.

To the shared experience of the European Founding Six, to their common experience of defeat, occupation and liberation in war, could be added the end of Empire, the return of the settlers and administrators to the European motherlands. Not surprisingly this added to the general feeling of loss of power and influence of the nation state that helped shape post-war political attitudes in Europe.

And Britain? Was not the end of Empire, the retreat to the mother country, an experience that Britain too shared? Was not the UK a member of the club of former imperial powers in Western Europe? Was not Britain now, shorn of Empire, just another middle-sized European nation state as its own Europhiles, repeatedly and almost lovingly assert?

And the answer is much closer to No than to Yes. It is indeed one of the many remarkable facts that contemporary historians and political commentators have failed to identify at least two of the rather singular characteristics of British overseas rule.

Of these, much the most important lies in the nature of so many of the territories that the British were to conquer and to settle: most notably, the 'New Worlds' of North America and Australasia, thinly populated as they were by nomadic and tribal peoples. No doubt assisted by the continued attrition of war and the still greater depredations wrought by European and English diseases, settlers from the British Isles rapidly outnumbered the indigenous peoples in those two continents. The American Colonies, at the time by far the largest of the British overseas settlements, broke free from British rule in their War of Independence in 1783 – and then threw open the doors to European settlement, almost unchecked throughout the nineteenth and early twentieth century. (The post-independence UK-US relationship is a subject to be examined later. But British people continued to settle in large numbers in Canada throughout that period. A similar process of British settlement took place in South Africa's Cape colony and Natal and with still larger numbers in Australia and New Zealand.)

Learning the lesson of the loss of the American colonies, Canada, South Africa, Australia and New Zealand were substantially self-governing by the mid-1850s, and were formally accepted as independent countries by the end of the century. When the League of Nations was launched in 1919, it included among its forty two original members Australia, Canada, New Zealand and South Africa. Their relationship with the United Kingdom was further defined in the 1935 Statute of Westminster. All recognised the British monarch as their Head of State – and all of them, by decisions of their respective parliaments, declared war on Germany following the British declaration on 3 September 1939.

The crucial point here is of course that the withdrawal from Empire, the going home of the colonial administrators, the military chiefs and the settlers that characterised the end of Empire for our Continental neighbours simply didn't happen – couldn't happen – in these closely related and predominantly British-populated territories. The UK remains therefore inescapably committed to and involved with strong English-speaking nation states in three of the six continents of the world.

A process of imperial withdrawal, closer to that experienced by mainland European countries, did take place with the end of the Indian Empire and the progressive withdrawal from colonial rule in much of Africa and elsewhere. This was an experience 'closer' to that of our European neighbours – but by no means identical.

Not least of the differences was in the manner of Britain's departure. Long before the Second World War, the British political class – with a few celebrated exceptions – had accepted that the empire must end; that colonial peoples had the right to self government and that democracy in the parliament of the imperial power would not permit continued coercive rule against the wishes of a subject people. These, without doubt, were the deeply held views and imperial withdrawal the policies of Her Majesty's then Opposition, the Labour Party. But they were held too by a substantial number of Conservative MPs. The 1935 India Act which ceded internal self-government and institutionalised democratic elections throughout India was, after all, passed by a Conservative government in the House of Commons. Elsewhere, in Africa particularly, the argument for self-government in principle was conceded. 'Not ready yet' was the not always honest argument for delay, but continued rule could only be justified if it was in preparation for ultimate self-government.

The 1935 Act did not go far enough for many Indian nationalists and the whole British-Indian relationship was placed under immense strain when the Indian National Congress adopted an anti-war policy in 1939 and organised nationwide passive resistance campaigns. In 1942, following the Japanese victory over the British and British-Indian armies in Burma, with Japanese troops on the borders of India itself, with the call for mass uprisings from Chandra Bose, one of the Congress leaders, with Nehru and Ghandi in prison, and the recruitment of a Japanese-supporting Indian National Army from prisoners of war, British India faced its greatest crisis.

But it survived. British and Indian forces broke the Japanese siege of Kohima and began the hard-fought reconquest of Burma. Churchill was astute enough to send Sir Stafford Cripps to India to open a new dialogue with Nehru, Ghandi and Jinnah about future independence – and whatever reservations Indian leaders still had about British intentions post-war vanished with Attlee's massive electoral victory in July 1945. The British withdrawal from India, only two years later, marred only by the communal carnage in the Punjab, was agreed and carried out in an atmosphere of friendship and trust. The British government, with remarkable wisdom, in 1946 pardoned *en masse* those who had joined the Japanese-recruited Indian National Army and had fought against us. No court martial, no condemnations, no bitter legacies.

The difference between the British withdrawal from India and the French and Dutch expulsion from Indo-China, Algeria and Indonesia could scarcely be more marked.

True, the institutional preparations that preceded independence – the laying of the foundation for elected government and the rule of law – were not always as successfully arranged in other parts of the British Empire. Kenya, Guyana, Sierra Leone and Cyprus did not escape bloodshed and strife. But they were the exceptions, not the rule. And so, one of the main prizes of peaceful withdrawal was the willing association of all previously ruled British territories – with the sole exception of Burma – with each other and with the UK in the Commonwealth of Nations. The Commonwealth embraces now some fifty four independent nation states, fifty two of which were formerly parts of the British Empire. In population terms, they total 1.5 billion, one quarter of mankind. The role and future of the Commonwealth will be discussed later but, far from being a fading memory of Britain's imperial past, the Commonwealth shows every sign of growing influence and activity and of developing its own separate identity – so much so that two of the nations that have most recently joined, Mozambique and the Cameroons, were never British territories.

The relationship between the old imperial power and its now independent and assertive ex-colonies was not without difficulties and tensions. The UK's greatest single act of folly, in the post-war period, Suez, was roundly condemned, either in public or in private, by virtually all Commonwealth countries – except Australia. But the longest-lasting cause of division and bitterness within the Commonwealth, one that largely isolated the UK, was continued white minority rule in South Africa. South Africa itself was a senior member of the Commonwealth. South African troops had fought alongside the British in many theatres of war, most memorably in the Western Desert. Then, disastrously, in 1947 South Africa voted for Dr Malan's National Party, a party dedicated to permanent white minority rule and to the deeply offensive policies of racial separation and discrimination – apartheid. Britain, with its historical connections with South Africa and its strategically placed naval base at Simonstown was undoubtedly not anxious to bring matters to a head – and its reluctance to do so was severely criticised by its other Commonwealth partners, increasingly in the 1960s and 70s as the Commonwealth was joined by newly independent African states. Under bitter attack, South Africa withdrew from the Commonwealth in 1962.

But the issue then moved on to the question of arms supply and trade sanctions, which the UK was reluctant to impose.

Even more seriously, because the Central African Federation was not yet an independent country, the coupling together of white-dominated Southern Rhodesia with the adjacent colonies of Northern Rhodesia and Nyasaland, seemed to most observers and certainly to most Commonwealth countries to be a further and calculated extension of white supremacist rule – a development under Britain's direct control.

Ian Smith's unilateral declaration of independence (UDI) in 1965 brought the issue to world attention. Commonwealth countries demanded British intervention to suppress the revolt and claimed that only racism in Britain prevented the necessary action. At the same time in Britain itself, there was a sudden awakening to the fact that substantial Commonwealth immigration, principally from the West Indies and the Indian subcontinent, was turning Britain into a multiracial society – with little understanding of the problems, prejudices and anxieties such a development entails.

UDI in white supremacist Rhodesia almost coincided with Enoch Powell's famous speech, with its dark foreboding that 'rivers of blood' would flow in the streets of our cities unless immigration was brought to a halt. The recently formed Labour government of Harold Wilson, strongly led by the Prime Minister, reacted by legislating against racial discrimination and incitement to racial hatred in the UK, held continued direct face-to-face meetings with Ian Smith and organised economic sanctions against Southern Rhodesia. But Wilson would not use force and his refusal to do so led to memorably bitter Commonwealth Heads of Government meetings, where British inaction was generally condemned and in particular pilloried by Tanganyika's Nyerere and Zambia's Kenneth Kaunda – the so-called Front Line states.

At the worst period in the 1960s, pessimists might well have predicted the break-up of the Commonwealth, along divisive racial lines. In the 1960s and in the 1970s and into the 1980s as well, a large majority of the Commonwealth countries were preoccupied, to the near exclusion of all other concerns, with fighting racism and colonialism in general and in particular, with understandable vehemence, white racist rule in Rhodesia and South Africa.

Far from drawing support and enhancing its influence from the numerically growing New Commonwealth, Britain found itself often isolated and indeed the target for attack not only in Commonwealth forums but in those of the United Nations as well. With slowly growing economies, with large sterling debts accumulated during the war, still to be disposed of, many in Britain persuaded themselves that the Commonwealth was a wasting asset, a burden on Britain's overstretched resources. All of this – together with the abandonment of democracy in a number of the New Commonwealth countries and the odious reverse racism of Idi Amin's Uganda – affected political opinion and media comment in the crucial years after 1959, when the Macmillan government lost its nerve and made the first abortive effort to join the Common Market.

Not all British Leaders were so persuaded. Most notably Hugh Gaitskell, then Leader of the Opposition Labour Party, as mentioned above, rejected the case for joining the Common Market in his famous conference speech in Brighton in 1962 largely on the grounds that Membership would damage the vital economic interests of Commonwealth countries and at the same time undermine the independence of the United Kingdom itself. His successor, Harold Wilson, held very similar views at the time but was unhappily to abandon them in the period of his own Premiership after 1964. Henceforth, the interests of the Commonwealth would cease to be a dominating concern for Britain's political leaders.

But, once again, in their negative assessment of the New Commonwealth as much as with their failure to understand the unique character of the Old, the Europhiles got it wrong. Instead of the white-supremacy conflict finally tearing the Commonwealth apart, the problem itself was soon to be vastly eased in Southern Rhodesia and the Central African Federation in 1979-80, when the newly appointed Governor Soames, following the Lancaster House Conference, presided in Salisbury over the (brilliantly negotiated and organised) temporary return to the legitimacy of British rule there – to be shortly followed by guerrilla disarmament, country-wide elections and full independence.

South Africa had to wait another decade before President De Klerk made his decisive move, to release Nelson Mandela from over twenty years of imprisonment and to open the dialogue that, in a few years, was to end political apartheid and bring about the formation of a new government under the newly-elected – by universal suffrage – President Nelson Mandela. In the decade that lay between Southern

Rhodesia's (Zimbabwe's) independence and Mandela's release, the Southern African political landscape had been further transformed by the end of Portuguese colonial rule in the great adjacent territories of Angola and Mozambique – a major event but one which unhappily was accomplished only after a bloody and prolonged conflict, much of which has continued ever since.

With the solution to the Southern Rhodesian problem obtained, and Mandela released from his Island captivity, Commonwealth leaders were free to turn their minds to matters other than the great question of race. Appropriately, it was in Harare, formerly Salisbury the renamed capital of Zimbabwe, that the 1991 Commonwealth Heads of Government Meeting, the CHOGM, gave itself a new and defining political role the promotion of democracy, good government and human rights throughout its fifty-member association. The new Harare Declaration did not fail to include traditional concerns for promoting racial equality and for sustainable economic growth. But at the heart of the Declaration was a new commitment to democracy: 'To the protection and promotion of the fundamental political values of the Commonwealth: democracy, democratic procedures and institutions which reflect national circumstances and the rule of law and the independence of the judiciary, just and honest government; fundamental human rights, including equal rights and opportunities of all their citizens regardless of race, class, creed or political belief'.

Of equal importance was the decision – also universally agreed – of the 1995 CHOGM in Auckland, New Zealand to 'fulfil more effectively the commitment contained in the Harare Commonwealth Declaration' by setting up an Action Programme, under the control of the Secretary General of the Commonwealth and eight nominated Commonwealth Foreign Ministers, 'to take appropriate steps to maintain democracy by means of all kinds, including election observer teams and, where democracy has been overthrown, steps necessary to ensure its restoration'.

The first targets of the latter were defined in December 1995 as Nigeria, The Gambia and Sierra Leone. Of course the Commonwealth has limited means. But no one should doubt that the censure of colleagues, the continuing watch over the practice of democracy and regard for human rights, the threat of suspension, ultimately expulsion from the Commonwealth itself and the possibility of sanctions, do carry considerable weight with those in the Commonwealth dock. Military rule ended in Nigeria in 1999, when elected government was restored in February. The Gambia has greatly improved its governmental practices and invited the Ministerial Action Group to assess at first hand the acceptance there of the Harare principles. Sierra Leone remains in turmoil in spite of the negotiated Lome Peace Agreement and the stationing there of a substantial UN Peace-Keeping Force. Indeed, it needed the arrival of heavily armed British ground, naval and air forces in May 2000 to prevent internal collapse and a humiliating setback to the authority of the United Nations.

The military coup in Pakistan in November 1999 met with immediate Commonwealth censure at the Durban CHOGM in South Africa, and the suspension of Pakistan from membership. Further demands include the release of the former Prime Minister and for the military to set a date for the restoration of democracy and civil rule.

Other Commonwealth countries, including Zimbabwe, Kenya, Zambia and Sri Lanka, know that they are under the critical scrutiny of their colleagues. June 2000 saw the renewed suspension of Fiji from the Commonwealth and strong Commonwealth pressure on the Solomon Islands.

In Zimbabwe, the Commonwealth faced a severe test of its commitment to democracy when in the spring of 2000, with the approach of Parliamentary general elections, President Mugabe began his systematic campaign to intimidate the main Opposition Party and encourage the so-called veterans to seize and occupy unlawfully the land of white farmers known to be the Opposition's supporters. The Commonwealth Secretary General visited Harare in May and teams of Commonwealth election observers are to watch over the June elections there.

Considering how recently most Commonwealth countries have acquired their independence and self-government and how understandabl, sensitive newly independent nations tend to be about interference in their internal affairs, these are remarkable and most welcome developments – developments with which the UK is itself wholly at ease.

The 1999 Durban meeting ended with a further Commonwealth decision of considerable potential importance: the setting up of a High Level Group to review the role of the Commonwealth in the twenty-first century – and to report back to the next Australian CHOGM in 2001.

This process of widening, defining and strengthening the role of the Commonwealth while wholly acceptable to the UK, owes little to British pressure and initiative. The inactivity and indeed deliberate distancing of Britain from the Commonwealth since we joined the Common Market in 1973, and even in the preparatory years before that event, has been one of the most extraordinary – but little observed – developments in our national policy.

Trade and investment statistics relating to the UK and the Commonwealth countries, either bilaterally or as a whole, are no longer systematically compiled. Yet – this is one more changed aspect of the contemporary Commonwealth – dynamic economic growth, so welcome a feature in the 'tiger economies' in much of South East Asia, is an increasingly marked feature in a number of Commonwealth economies as well. Malaysia and the Island states of Mauritius, the Bahamas, Trinidad and Cyprus are well in the lead but, most hopeful of all – while its average per capita income is still very low – great city regions of India, including Bangalore, Bombay and Calcutta are surging ahead and with the most modern technologies. Singapore, almost unbelievably, has the highest per capita income of all Commonwealth countries – higher than Canada, Australia and the UK.

The UK has obvious assets and advantages in these markets. A shared language and similar business cultures and accountancy practices, together with investment accumulated over more than a century and a half, are advantages which no other European country enjoys.

Just over 50 per cent of Britain's trade is now undertaken with the European Union where it is fostered, not only by the preferential arrangements of the Common Market and the Single Market but by the encouragement of successive British governments. Nevertheless, of the UK trade conducted with the world outside of Europe at least 20 per cent is accounted for in our continued Commonwealth trade. Of very considerable significance for the future, no less than 29.3 per cent of the UK's direct foreign capital investment flows to the Commonwealth – as compared to just 13.6 per cent to the European Union. (European Union figures exclude only The Netherlands: major companies in that country, e.g. Unilever and Shell, reinvest in Third World countries rather than in the European mainland.)

Britain's overseas aid programme – like that of Canada and Australia – makes a significant contribution to the economic development of the poorer Commonwealth countries. India and Bangladesh are still large recipients. But the programme as a whole has been much reduced in the past two decades. Almost unbelievably, the Major government agreed in 1992 to transfer a large part of the UK's aid programme to the European Community for them to allocate, co-ordinate and combine with the contributions from other member states. Of our £2 billion per annum total overseas aid budgets, not less than £800 million a year is paid into the European Community to be then allocated, according to their priorities and their administrative procedures to the various aid recipients.

167

As the Secretary of State for International Development, Clare Short, said in an answer to a Parliamentary question on 3 February 1999 that she inherited a situation 'in which EC aid spending is both skewed against the poorest countries and often of poor quality'. In truth, next to the CAP, the European Community's aid programme is the most notoriously inefficient, not to say corrupt programme of the European Union.

Unhappily, this tale of culpable neglect by successive British governments of Britain's own interests and those of her most committed friends, is far from over. Those who can bear to study it, will find massive documentation in the House of Commons Foreign Affairs Select Committee's Report on *The Future Role of the Commonwealth* published in March 1996 – the first Select Committee study and report on the Commonwealth in the post-Common Market period. Among the more foolish government decisions have been the continued and short-sighted cuts in those UK programmes that have direct relevance to the Commonwealth: the imposition of full-cost fees on students from Commonwealth countries attending British Universities; the continuing pressure on the budgets of the BBC's World Service, in spite of the central need to develop a world TV service alongside its radio network; and the similar reductions in the expenditure plans of the British Council, with its network of libraries, information and teaching services. Present estimates are that nearly 170 million people outside the UK, but inside the Commonwealth, speak the English language and the World Service reaches 140 million of them.

Here are incomparably powerful instruments of cultural diplomacy which the meanest intelligence cannot fail to note. Yet the danger is real that the intellectual elite of many Commonwealth countries, in particular of India, are being priced out of British Universities and are attending instead those of the United States – where students have the opportunity and where the tradition exists –

of working their way through college. And there is the danger too that an under-resourced BBC television service will be overpowered and blotted out by the omnipresent CNN.

Select committees are not given to hyperbole but the Foreign Affairs Committee of 1996 (all-party, but with a Conservative majority) was driven by the evidence to state: 'We find the official approach to the activities of the two agencies [BBC World Service and the British Council] in question frankly incredible'.

Perhaps most damning of all has been the failure of successive UK governments to sustain, publicise and adequately resource those central Commonwealth institutions that are located here in London. All organisations need an ongoing presence, funding and full time personnel on the scale and of the calibre appropriate to their task. The headquarters of the Commonwealth is Marlborough House in London, presided over by the Commonwealth Secretary General, the former New Zealand Foreign Minister Don McKinnon since February 2000, and for more than a decade previously by the distinguished Nigerian Chief Anouku. The functions of the Commonwealth Secretariat include maintaining the ongoing network of contacts between the now fifty four member states including the UK. Beyond that is the duty of preparing and organising the annual Commonwealth Finance Ministers meeting – held in Washington on the eve of the annual meetings of the IMF and the World Bank there – the triennial meetings of Commonwealth Education Ministers and, by far the most important, the biannual summit of the Heads of Government, the CHOGM.

In between such meetings, the Secretariat can do as much – or as little – as member states demand and its resources allow. These include tasks as varied as the allocation among applicants of the much-appreciated Commonwealth Fund for Technical Co-operation, particularly helpful to the smaller Commonwealth states, the organisation of election monitoring teams and the provision of professional advice on debt management. Above all, the Commonwealth Secretariat is the natural focal point for the continuing evaluation and study of the myriad interests and problems that the Commonwealth countries share with each other and for the useful development, wherever possible, of joint positions in the numerous international and regional forums where they sit as members.

There is indeed substantial and worthwhile work to be done. And the resources? Total annual expenditure on the Secretariat itself is just over £10 million per annum, of which the UK finances about 30 per cent, some £3 million. There are of course the special programmes – the Commonwealth Funds for Technical Co-operation, the Commonwealth Science Council, the Commonwealth Youth Programme – but the whole operation, including the Secretariat, costs just £35 million per annum to which the UK contributes roughly £11 million. When one remembers that the UK's net subscription (that is its payment after receipts) to the Commission of the European Union – a subscription virtually halved from Edward Heath's original terms of entry, after nearly five years of demonic campaigning by Mrs Thatcher – is running at some £3 billion a year, one can only marvel at the near lunatic loss of any sense of proportion and political judgement that the two contrasting figures reveal.

As Malcolm Rifkind, then Secretary of State for Foreign Affairs was to tell the Commons Select Committee in his evidence: 'The Commonwealth provides an opportunity for us to influence the policies of many governments around the world ... we have an ability to influence events – sometimes profoundly, sometimes at the margins – in every continent of the world and that is very much in our national interest'.

Yet, in spite of such indifference and neglect, the Commonwealth remains not a fading relic or memory of a long-abandoned Empire, but as the most numerous, influential and geographically widely spread organisation outside the United Nations itself. Far from diminishing, the Commonwealth has transformed itself into a matrix of cross-linkages, spreading throughout the world into a free association of nations with natural regional leaders and with the UK retaining an influence, no more but certainly not less, than might be expected from the founder member who has the advantage of being, still, the richest member of the club. Moreover, the Commonwealth is an international grouping with its own distinct mission – to further the cause of democracy, of good government, human rights and the rule of law within its own ranks and in the world at large.

That is the Commonwealth today. Will it continue into the new century that has now opened before us? Almost certainly it will. Like all institutions, it will of course adapt and change. And its affairs do need much more intelligent and knowledgeable attention than the present Foreign Office and its Ministers have so far shown. The thuggery, and, worse directed against the white farmers and their black employees in Zimbabwe by Mugabe's supporters in the run-up to the general election there is a case in point. Britain's own protest certainly needed as wide a backing as we could muster. Yet it was not to the Commonwealth Secretary General nor to the specially appointed group of eight Commonwealth Foreign Ministers mandated at the Durban CHOGM that the UK turned – but to the European Union. This was a classic case for Commonwealth mediation and initiative and particularly for enlisting the support of the main African states of the Commonwealth. Yet it was not until the European Union's approaches had, predictably, failed and relations between Britain and Zimbabwe had fallen to an all-time low, that our Foreign Ministers remembered that Britain, like Zimbabwe, was a member of the Commonwealth, that Harare had been the location for the Commonwealth's main democracy and human rights statement, and asked the group of eight Commonwealth Ministers to send the Secretary General to Harare and to use their influence on Mugabe to pursue wiser and better policies.

In spite of this and no doubt other setbacks, the underlying reasons for optimism that the Commonwealth will strengthen and endure remain persuasive.

There is another factor, probably more potent than all the rest in cementing the Commonwealth together in the years ahead, that needs to be mentioned – a factor of which, once again, our contemporary historians and commentators seem to be blindly unaware: the continued reinforcement and refreshment of Commonwealth links through the movement of people in and out of the UK.

In the half century that has passed since the end of the Second World War, the outflow of British people emigrating to the old, independent dominions of Australia, Canada, New Zealand and – in spite of the great uncertainties there – South Africa has never ceased. More than a trickle, less than a flood, but a flow too strong and persistent to be ignored. To Australia, in the past half century, no less than 2 million British people have emigrated; over 1.1 million to Canada; 500,000 to South Africa and 450,000 to New Zealand. Of course, the flow has strengthened and eased in different post-war decades but in the last complete decade for which figures are available, 1985 to 1994, 252,000 British citizens set up home in Australia, 61,000 in Canada, 38,000 in South Africa and 37,000 in New Zealand. In the last few years, the British outflow has been running at, roughly 34,000 a year. Figures of the reverse traffic from these countries into the UK are not available but it is considerable, and with sensible schemes exempting, or partially exempting, from our otherwise stringent immigration controls Commonwealth citizens with family connections in the UK, it will certainly continue.

Once again, it is difficult to estimate how widespread those family connections are. But when one absorbs the fact that in the post-war half century, over 4 million British people have settled in these English-speaking lands, it would be surprising if less than one in three families in the UK have not close relatives (in their own, their parents or their grandparents' generations) in one or other of these countries.

Nor is migration confined – although it is certainly the largest of our overseas connections – to the old, self-governing Dominions. The same half century has seen the end of empire, beginning with the withdrawal from India in 1947. But the end of the Empire marked only the beginning of the settlement in substantial numbers in the UK itself of the peoples we had formerly ruled. Very substantial emigration began in the mid-1950s, during the years when no controls were placed by the UK on Commonwealth immigrants. The 1961 Act changed that but it placed a check, rather than a stop, on the immigrant flow. Large immigrant communities from the Caribbean and the Indian subcontinent, and smaller ones from Nigeria and elsewhere, were formed in those years, with settlements concentrated in most of the major cities in the UK – particularly in those areas where shortage of labour made job opportunities readily available. According to our latest Census of Population, there are now residing in the UK five hundred thousand from the countries of the Caribbean, nine hundred thousands from India, six hundred thousands from Pakistan and two hundred thousands from Bangladesh – and with people, no less from the New Commonwealth as from the Old, come connections, understandings, interests and involvement in the countries whence they came. Moreover, these links with the countries of origin, in this age of air travel, are more frequently refreshed than in any previous period of history. In one of those statements of the obvious that never cease to surprise, the then Minister of State at the FCO, Lynda Chalker, told the House of Commons Select Committee: 'In Europe we are one in fifteen. In the Commonwealth we are one of 51'.

But it is not just numbers that make the difference. The real point is that there is no other country in the world, and certainly not in the

European Union, that has the same deep, ongoing connection with other countries and continents that the UK possesses.

The World Outside II

The USA and the UN

No review of Britain's place in the world and the prospects before us as the new century unfolds, could fail to appraise our relationships with the world's strongest nation, the United States and with the wider international community of which we are a part.

The United States is of course one of our major trade partners, accounting for 16 per cent and 17 per cent of our visible exports and imports. More important than these volumes are undoubtedly our bilateral trade in invisibles and the massive capital investment that we already posses and continue to enhance in each other's economies: not only direct investment but massive portfolio investment by insurance companies, pension funds and other institutional investors channelled into the vast equity and bond markets of Wall Street and the City of London. And from America – although it is again a two-way traffic – product innovation, managerial skills and business-school expertise flow freely, and beneficially, into the United Kingdom's economy.

But important as trade and investment are, it is the US influence in world affairs, security and defence that matter most. Looking back over the twentieth century, the United States has indeed played a crucial role in foreign and defence affairs. It was America's entry, late as it was, into the First World War that decisively tilted the balance of power in favour of the Allies and ended what at times seemed the never-ending carnage of that four-year conflict. In the Second World War, no one should question the parts played by Britain, the Commonwealth and by the Soviet Union in resisting and defeating Hitler's Germany. But it was again American power, not only the huge armed forces that America eventually mobilised but also the massive output of armaments from American industry that was the crucial factor in Germany's defeat. And it was, once more, the strength of the American economy, the scale of its weapons production, the presence, organisation and fighting power of its military forces, together with its development of nuclear weapons, the means of delivering them and her space technology, that successfully contained and ultimately broke Soviet power in the more than forty years' struggle, the Cold War, that began almost as soon as the Second World War ended.

Against such a background – and there are many other aspects of the relationship to be noted – it is hardly surprising that British leaders have placed the highest value on the American alliance. History does teach lessons, even when its students are not very anxious to learn them. One very painful lesson was the reversion of the United States to its traditional neutralism after its decisive intervention in the First World War. Virtual withdrawal of the United States from international events, its opting out of membership in the League of Nations, made it all too easy in the inter-war years for the aggressor states to have their way. So, in the 1930s, Japan was able to attack China; Nazi Germany, Austria and Czechoslovakia; Italy, Ethiopia and Albania.

Not surprisingly it became a central aim of the United Kingdom, beginning with Churchill and followed by Attlee and virtually all their successors, after the Second World War, to involve the United States permanently in the defence and reconstruction of Western Europe – and more widely in world affairs. It was indeed a crucial moment when an overstretched Britain in 1947 had to announce the forthcoming withdrawal of British troops from Greece, when that country was still under extreme pressure from communist guerrillas backed by hostile communist neighbour states. America, in the process of rapid demobilisation and disengagement, had to make a historic decision. The answer came in the President's February 1947 speech, subsequently known as the Truman Doctrine, committing United States to the defence of democracy against aggression everywhere. Later events, the Berlin airlift conducted by British and American transport planes, the American Marshall Plan, so swiftly and effectively taken forward by the then British Foreign Secretary Ernest Bevin, the formation of NATO in 1949, together these achieved the United Kingdom's twin post-war aims: the commitment of the United States to the economic reconstruction of war-torn Europe and the long-term involvement of both Canadian and American troops on the ground whose tasks included the defence of the United Kingdom.

America's relationships with other European countries developed and intensified during these years. Indeed, as we have previously recounted, a dominant school in the State Department, backed by Secretaries of State and Presidents, with more or less enthusiasm, was an advocate of European Unity and gave support to the various initiatives taken to achieve that end. Some influential American leaders, most notably Dean Acheson and John Foster Dulles, openly pressed and advocated UK membership of the new European structures – the European Coal and Steel Community, the European Defence Community and the Rome Treaty.

Nevertheless, in the post-war years, there was undeniably a different relationship between the US and the UK, closer and more wide-ranging, than that which existed between the US and other European nations. To an important extent, the wartime alliance made certain of that – and many arrangements made then have continued throughout the post-war years. (Most notably, these include collaboration in the development of nuclear weapons, the supply of long-range missile delivery systems and the collection, processing and analysis of intelligence gathered from installations in the United Kingdom itself as well as from British overseas territories.) Inevitably, even within the NATO Alliance, there was – and is – an extra intimacy between the US and the UK, in nuclear strategy, in nuclear weapon deployment and in shared military and political intelligence.

But the Anglo-American Alliance – a term which I prefer to the somewhat loose and sentimental 'special relationship' – has deeper roots and a much wider scope than NATO membership, important as that is. The US is indeed a world power. Its physical, military presence is there in Japan and on many island bases across the Pacific; in South Korea, US power, presence and interests are on the Asian mainland itself. In addition, the United States is a major player in the Middle East and retains its traditional involvement and leadership in South America. The US is therefore constantly involved in political, economic and strategic developments virtually worldwide. No other country can begin to match their power and global reach. But there is one nation that can almost match the United States not in power but in global interest and connections and with diplomatic skills at least equal to her own: the United Kingdom. In some areas indeed, in the Indian subcontinent and in Australasia, the UK's connections are probably stronger and more intimate than those of the United States.

And it is not just worldwide reach and contacts that we have in common. There are shared political values as well. The thrust of US policy is inevitably influenced by the values of its own democracy, by its belief in government by the people, and in the rule of law. It is therefore most at ease with – and has a natural tendency to back and sustain – regimes of a similar kind elsewhere.

The strength of that tendency should not be exaggerated. As the past half-century has shown on several unhappy occasions, American foreign policy – and that of the UK as well – has befriended, at least for a time, undemocratic and authoritarian regimes. But the end of the Cold War and the sharp reduction in America's almost obsessive fear of Communism, has helped restore balance to American diplomacy and the tilt towards democracy can be clearly seen. In Latin America, in particular, in America's own 'backyard', before the Berlin wall came down, there was hardly a single country that was not governed by an overtly military or military-backed authoritarian regime. A decade later, not one is left. Britain itself contributed – by accident rather than by design – when the successful expedition to reclaim the Falklands from Argentina inflicted a humiliating defeat on Galtieri's military regime, which led to its collapse and replacement by democratic rule. But American diplomacy and economic assistance has been assiduously at work throughout the continent, promoting the restoration of democracy everywhere.

Here indeed, in the promotion of democracy, we have a shared, global enterprise – one in which the UK has a great deal to contribute and which will be shared with, and strengthened by, the post-Harare Commonwealth.

The other great global cause that we share with the United States is to uphold, protect and enforce the fundamental principles of international relationships – the principles embedded in the United Nations Charter, the Charter that Britain and America largely co-authored in 1944-5 – that outlaws aggression and renounces the use of force in settling disputes between nations.

And so, from the beginning of the post-war era, Britain and America have found themselves in partnership worldwide, either in joint military operations or in strong diplomatic and arms supply support of each other, in resisting aggressors and aggression. The deliberate, carefully planned assault of the Russian-equipped army of North Korea on its neighbour across the 38th Parallel in 1950 triggered the first major combined operation of American and

British forces, outside the European mainland. Under the UN flag, British troops and Royal Navy units fought alongside the Americans in that prolonged, difficult, but ultimately successful conflict. In 1982, it was America that supplied air missiles for British planes, satellite intelligence and strong diplomatic support during the Falklands campaign against the Argentina. In 1986, it was from British air bases that American planes struck their punitive blow against Colonel Gadaffi and his terrorist- sponsoring regime in Libya.

More important still, it was overwhelmingly the United States, but with the support of the United Kingdom, and at arms length from their main bases that assembled, the great number of ground troops, aircraft and naval vessels necessary to defeat the armed forces of Iraq and to expel them from Kuwait in 1991. The cynical can say that the motivation was oil. Oil may have played a part but it was much more than that. It was the first crucial decision, in the post-Cold War world, to insist upon obedience to the most fundamental of all the tenets: that unprovoked aggression by one state upon another cannot be allowed and that the victim state must be rescued and the aggressor punished by the collective armed strength of the world community, led by the permanent members of the United Nations Security Council. In this vital and testing decision to uphold the rule of law outside the European Continent it was striking that, America apart, it was only Britain among the European nations that gave wholehearted diplomatic as well as military support to defeating Iraq and to winning the Gulf War. The United Kingdom has of course had a long history of involvement, economic, diplomatic and military, in the whole Gulf area, and continues to exercise more influence with the Gulf states there and to have closer relationships with Saudi Arabia than any other European state. France did, it is true, send some naval and ground forces to the Gulf, but French diplomacy, very active in Baghdad and in other Arab capitals, seemed designed not so much to pressure Iraq for immediate withdrawal from Kuwait, as to show Saddam Hussein that he had a more sympathetic ear in Paris than anywhere else in the non-Arab world.

In the latter part of the 1990s, as post-Communist Yugoslavia fell apart and Belgrade sought to impose Serbian authority over other parts of that dissolving state, the US, Britain and other West European nations intervened first through the United Nations to organise relief supplies and establish safe areas and then through diplomatic initiatives to give international recognition to the newly-created mini-states of Slovenia, Croatia and Macedonia. Only in Bosnia was NATO, with American air power, brought into action. The Dayton Accords and patched-up truce that then ensued remain uneasily in place. But in 1998-9 the Serbs unleashed harsh repressive measures against the Albanian Kosovars in their southernmost province – leading to much bloodshed and killing, the flight of urban populations into the surrounding hills and a still larger flight of Albanian Kosovars across the frontiers into Albania itself and Macedonia. NATO's response was to confront Serbia with demands to desist and withdraw; then, faced with Milosevic's intransigence, the great air assault was launched and sustained against Kosovo and Serbia itself. It was again the assembly and use of American air power and the very strong political leadership of the British Prime Minister that were the decisive factors in the ultimate withdrawal of the Serbs from Kosovo and the return of the refugees there.

Shortly after, just before the end of the year 1999, in tiny East Timor the United Nations and Western diplomatic pressure finally forced the Indonesian government to hold there a referendum on independence. When the verdict for separation was overwhelmingly registered, armed Indonesian mobs, with the connivance if not support of Indonesian troops, let loose a campaign of murder, expulsion, burning and looting throughout the territory. UN intervention was demanded – and obtained. But this time the lead power was

Australia, the principal Commonwealth power in that geographical area, backed up with small contingents from many other Commonwealth countries including the UK. No doubt the UK could have sent more than a few companies of Ghurkas if the great majority of our mobile forces were not already engaged in policing Kosovo. Of course, apart from Portugal, the former colonial government of East Timor, no EU forces were involved.

Given the background of comradeship in arms and in mutually supportive diplomacy both in the great conflicts of the twentieth century and in the cold war that ensued, and given their shared endeavours not just in Europe but worldwide, it is hardly surprising that on both sides of the Atlantic the feeling exists that there is an overlap of interest and a stronger bond joining the UK and the US, different from that which the US has with other European nations. It is this that leads many observers to note that, in political terms, the Channel is wider than the Atlantic.

The English language plays a significant part too. This certainly helps the ease of discourse, not only between British and American citizens whenever they meet, but in the continuing exchanges that take place between the politicians and professionals of both countries. The House of Commons has dozens of single country, all-Party Parliamentary Groups, which maintain contact and deepen understanding between Britain and other nations all over the world. But, by an order of magnitude, the British-American Parliamentary Group is by far the largest: no less than 629 parliamentarians – 402 from the House of Commons, 227 from the Lords – are in membership. There is too a very inexact but meaningful identification of Labour and Liberal with the Democrats, Conservative with the Republican Party, but what has been a surprisingly frequent phenomenon in the Anglo-American relationship is the personal chemistry that seems to have been felt by so many political leaders: Churchill and Roosevelt; Attlee and Truman; Macmillan and Kennedy; Thatcher and Reagan;

Blair and Clinton. Indeed, looking back on the whole period from the Second World War to date, I can think of only one British Prime Minister, Edward Heath, who felt neither personal warmth for his opposite number in the White House (admittedly, Richard Nixon was not to everyone's taste) nor the sense of continuing and shared political purpose. The cultural links provided by the output of Hollywood and the much smaller British film industry, the interchange of TV and radio programmes are important, and ongoing. So too is the transatlantic interchange of music, fashion, the arts and styles. Nor should we overlook the important part played by those great endowments, the Rhodes and Fulbright scholarships, that have brought to Britain's most famous universities young people of outstanding ability from the US – and elsewhere in the English-speaking world. Here they have gained an insight into (and generally affection for) the UK which has been of great help when, years later, they have occupied posts – like President Clinton – of the highest importance in government.

The Anglo-American connection goes far wider and deeper than the political and intellectual classes of the two countries. There is something about the famous classlessness and informality of relationships in the United States that strongly appeals to most Brits and equally, the personal restraint, the politeness and idiosyncrasy of the Brits has a special appeal to many Americans. Culture and personal relations obviously help in sustaining the Alliance. Yet they are not the decisive factors. There is no room for sentimentality in assessing the Anglo-American relationship. The interests of the UK and of the US do not always converge – and where they conflict the US certainly, the UK generally, will pursue their own perceived national interests. But, apart from the extraordinary British aberration that was Suez in 1956 and the tragically misjudged US military involvement in Vietnam, the world outlook and policies of the two nations and their governments have been remarkably similar. Democracy at home and the rule of law, and, abroad, the values of self determination and resistance to armed state aggression have indeed been the shared possessions of the two powers. Their application to the post-war world, imperfect as it has been, has nevertheless been a major factor in securing peace, freedom and decent government.

What stands out so clearly, and this bears repeating, from the half-century's history is that, outside the European Continent – and to some extent within it as well – the only partner America has in global management is the United Kingdom; and that the Continental allies in NATO, while they possess substantial resources and a still larger, though unmobilised potential, are almost wholly Eurocentric in their aims and concerns. It is of course this narrow Eurocentric focus, the absence of global involvement, that gives the new ambition of the European Union to forge a common foreign and security policy such a dangerous potential. Now that the single currency has been obtained, at least by the initial eleven, the next great target for the Europhiles is the development of a common foreign, security and defence policy for the European Union.

As mentioned earlier, security from external attack has been enjoyed for more than fifty years by the peoples and countries of Western Europe – and it has been secured above all by their membership of the 1949 North Atlantic Treaty. The essence of the treaty is that all its members are pledged to assist each other with armed collective might, if any member state comes under external attack. What turns it from a declaration of intent into a deterrent power of unmatched strength is the membership of the United States and the command and control organisation it has established in NATO's Brussels headquarters. A very important feature of NATO is that the bulk of the armed forces available from the European Continent, including those of Germany, are under American-led, multi-national, rather than national control.

NATO is essentially a *defence* pact, designed to provide collective security to its members. As such, it is almost by definition unlikely and unsuited to be deployed, militarily, on other tasks even within its own geographical Atlantic-European area.

Nevertheless, since the end of the cold war, NATO has gone well outside its original defence pact role. That limitation was breached, first by the intervention in Bosnia in 1995 and second, and more seriously, by the war over Kosovo in 1999. The implication of these developments, the precedents created, are matters of very considerable importance and concern – among them that it lacked in Kosovo the authorisation of the Security Council of the United Nations. But, while the United States played once again the major military role, its obvious and understandable reluctance to commit ground troops on the edges of Europe, did impose some constraint upon the whole exercise; not least in importance was the assessment of the risks involved with Russia – Serbia's long-established friend and protector from external attack.

What the champions of the European Union are now espousing is the de facto separation from NATO of a new European autonomous military capability, with its own command and control organisation, free to make decisions on the use of its military resources *without* the consent of the United States and Canada. Before NATO was formed in 1949, the British government of the day had negotiated a defence alliance with France and The Netherlands in the so-called Brussels Treaty. This created the Western European Union. It has continued a somewhat shadowy existence ever since, except for a brief high-profiled emergence in 1953 when, following the collapse of the European Defence Community proposal, Prime Minister Sir Anthony Eden pledged through the WEU to maintain four divisions of British troops on the continent of Europe into the twenty first century. The 1997 Amsterdam Treaty carried forward the European defence project by stating in terms, in a treaty protocol, that the European

Union and the WEU would draw up plans for a merger of the two bodies to make the WEU. the military arm of the European Union.

The implications for NATO of this development are clear. And one of Prime Minister Blair's principal claims for the success of his 'constructive approach' to the European Union when he came to power was the specific exemption in the Amsterdam Treaty from any European Union defence force of Britain and those other member states of the European Union who 'saw their main defence in NATO'.

As the relevant clause in the Amsterdam Treaty, clause J.7 puts it: 'The policy of the Union in accordance with this article will not prejudice the specific character of the security and defence policies of certain member states which see their common defence, realised in NATO, under the North Atlantic Treaty and be compatible with the common security and defence policy established within that framework'.

Returning to London on 18 June 1999, in confident, virtually triumphalist mood, Prime Minister Blair spoke about the goal of strengthening the European Union Foreign Policy co-operation and then, specifically on defence, declared that the goal: 'Will not be achieved through merging the European Union and the WEU or developing an unrealistic common defence policy. We therefore resisted its unacceptable proposals from others. Instead, we argued for – and won – the explicit recognition, written into the treaty for the first time, that NATO is the foundation of our and other allies' common defence'.

Challenged by John Major, then leading from the Opposition, to make clarity crystal clear when the treaty text referred to 'the possibility of the integration of the WEU into the EU' and to the claim made by the Dutch Presidency that 'for the first time, Britain had conceded the principle of integrating defence in the European Union', the Prime Minister gave an unambiguous response. On the issue of gradual integration of the EU and WEU he said: 'The draft treaty text was precisely what was changed so we now have a situation where there is no obligation to move into integration at all. That is the very thing we managed to secure'.

In a later exchange he was able to give the then Liberal Leader, Paddy Ashdown, the assurance that 'while common defence and a common defence policy was '*actually contemplated* in the Maastricht Treaty', he had gained the insertion of those words that 'made clear that the *UK saw its future defence* not *in the European Union but in* NATO'.

The Prime Minister was clear enough in June 1997. What events influenced him, what pressures were brought to bear, whether the desire to be – and to be seen to be – at the heart of Europe when the UK could not risk immediate commitment to the single currency. Whether separately or collectively these considerations gave the development of a common defence policy a particular attraction, no one has yet been able to discover or explain. But the fact of Mr Blair's could not have been made clearer than in the Joint Declaration issued at the end of the St Malo Summit meeting with France's President Chirac in December 1998. Coming within days of Chirac's successful meeting with Chancellor Schroeder in Potsdam (under the six-monthly bilateral arrangements of the Franco-German Treaty, on the eve of the German Presidency where the two leaders had pledged support for the further development of a European Union defence policy) the St Malo agreement carried the extra weight of the implicit German approval.

As the Joint Declaration of 4 December proclaimed: 'The European Union needs to be in a position to play its full role on the international stage ... to this end, the Union must have the capacity for autonomous action, backed up by credible military force, the means to decide to use them and a readiness to do so.'

As though to remove any possibility of doubt that actions, excluding the US and outside of NATO were not clearly in mind, the Joint Declaration asserted: 'The European Union will also need to have recourse to suitable military means. (European capabilities pre-designated within NATO's European pillar or national or multinational European means outside the NATO framework)'.

The extraordinary reversal of British policy in the eighteen months that separate the Treaty of Amsterdam in June 1997 from the St Malo Declaration in December 1998 occurred *before*, not after, the Kosovo war that was to begin some four months later. Kosovo cannot therefore be pressed into service as an explanation of unexpected events leading to a major policy change.

No; a single European foreign policy, backed up by an autonomous military capacity, under European control is now one of – if not the major – European initiatives at the centre of the Labour government's European policy. Indeed, at both the Cologne Heads of Government European Council in June 1999 and at the Helsinki European Council in December 1999, the project has been carried still further forward. At Helsinki, the European Union Heads of Government Council agreed to a 2003 target date for assembling a European Union force of between 50,000 to 60,000 troops, capable of carrying out a range of tasks, including the key peace enforcement task, and available for a minimum twelve-month period.

To the charge – of which he had himself been so conscious and was so anxious to refute in June 1997 – that these European Union arrangements could have adverse affects on NATO, the PM now claimed that 'as a result of our participation, it is moving in a clear direction, reinforcing NATO, not in opposition to it' and somewhat disingenuously confused the European Defence project with the undoubted wish of the United States that the European Alliance should take on a greater part of the NATO defence burden.

These arrangements have still to be clarified and developed: the degree of autonomy for the newly created EU force and the precise relationship with NATO will both be very important in coming to a serious judgement on the implications of the whole development.

But the extent and nature of UK – and United States – concern must now be stated. At least three authoritative US spokesmen have addressed the issue directly. One was Strobe Talbott, the US Deputy Secretary of State at a Chatham House Conference on the Future of NATO last October. Having stressed earlier the general American support for a more effective European military capability to deal with minor challenges to European security 'well before they reach the threshold of triggering US combat involvement', and clearly envisaging the availability of pre-identified NATO assets for limited European purposes, he expressed the major American reservation in these words: 'We would not want to see a European Security and Defence Initiative that comes into being first within NATO and then grows out of NATO and finally grows away from NATO, since that would lead to an ESDI that initially duplicates NATO but that could eventually compete with NATO'.

That was not all. Addressing himself specifically to the St Malo Joint Declaration and statement made at the end of the European Union's Cologne Heads of Government Council in June 1999, Mr Talbott expressed US concern that St Malo might exclude non-EU NATO Allies from the EU's planning and decision-making structures and that the Cologne declaration 'could be read to imply Europe's default position would be to act *outside* the Alliance whenever possible, rather than *through* the Alliance'.

The second voice to give public expression to American concerns was that of General Wesley Clark, Supreme Allied Commander NATO, interviewed by the *New York Times* in December 1999. As the General put it: 'The main American concern ... is de-coupling or duplication or discrimination against non-EU European members of NATO'.

The third American to express serious reservations about the autonomous European Union defence capability was the American Senator Gordon Smith, Chairman of the US Senate's European

Affairs Committee, in a speech in London on 10 December 1999. While expressing the wish for a stronger European pillar *within* NATO, the Senator made clear his opposition to the 'unnecessary duplication' of existing capabilities that would be involved in creating an *autonomous* European Union military capability and to the whole notion of the 'forging of a European Union into an *alternative* military Alliance in order to oppose the United States'.

Clearly there are a number of real problems for both the United States and the United Kingdom arising from the development of a separate European defence force, a separate European Union-controlled army. European forces do need substantial reinforcing and reshaping following the end of the Cold War. Change is needed both to make the European pillar of NATO more effective in military terms – above all more mobile and more rapidly deployable – and the imbalance in cost, effort and effectiveness between the United States and her European partners in NATO needs to be rectified.

But this can be accomplished without massive increases in military expenditure on the duplication of expensive equipment, provided it is done *within* NATO. NATO assets can be pre-assigned for limited European use in those – unlikely – circumstances where both the United States and the European Allies agree to limited all-European action. But two points need emphasis: the first is a prior agreement within NATO, agreement with the United States, that separate European Union action is appropriate; and the second that new defence forces are not organised *outside* NATO whose deployment would be separately decided by the institutions of the European Union.

It is hardly surprising that doubt and concern should exist on this very crucial point. The St Malo Joint Declaration, as already noted, in its final sentence in brackets at the end of its paragraph III – after stating that the European Union required 'suitable military means' to back up its external policies – specifically mentions both pre-designated capabilities *within* NATO or 'national or multi-national European means *outside* the NATO framework'.

This appears to be in sharp contrast to the Strategic Concept adopted by the Heads of Government at the fiftieth anniversary meeting of the North Atlantic Council in Washington on 23-24 April 1999, a few months after the St Malo meeting and Declaration. Here the NATO leaders declared that: 'The Alliance fully supports the development of the European Security and Defence Initiative (ESDI) *within* the Alliance by making available its assets and capabilities for WEU-led operations'. No mention of the key words in the St Malo Joint Declaration's paragraph III (European means *outside* the NATO framework).

As though to drive home the point of difference, the NATO Strategic Concept goes on to state that: 'On the basis of decisions taken by the Alliance in Berlin in 1996 and subsequently, the European Security and Defence Initiative will continue to be developed *within* NATO. This process will require a close co-operation between NATO, the WEU and, if and when appropriate, the European Union'.

Clearly, the US and many of its partners in NATO support a stronger European pillar based on the ESDI, in the Atlantic Alliance. But they see this emerging through building up the WEU and only 'if and when appropriate' by co-operating with the European Union.

Since the UK government is promoting the European Union defence project, it is most anxious to reassure the Americans that their worries are unfounded. Ministerial statements therefore stress the government's view that separate European Union defence deployment would be 'limited' to carrying out the so-called Petersburg Tasks. These do indeed include minor to moderate defence involvement's such as protecting the delivery of relief and aid supplies, separation of combatants and armed policing. But they also specifically embrace 'peace enforcement' – the contemporary euphemism for waging war.

Moreover, it is clear from the start that the European Union envisages not just using NATO assets for limited European Union operations but something much grander and all-embracing.

The Cologne Heads of Government Council in June 1999 made the crucial decision to set up a new political-military command structure, including a new Political and Security Committee, a European Military Committee and a supporting European Military Staff Committee.

Two particularly important components in the new European Defence capability are the availability of military air transport of appropriate size and a European intelligence-gathering facility. Both are costly. The first, transport, could be met by purchasing the proven American C17 Globe Masters – or by the all-European A400M, yet to be built. The latter would have the active support of all the European aircraft manufacturers, including British Aerospace, involved in Air Bus Military, the prospective manufacturer of the A4007 – and the purchase could, regardless of competitive advantages, be regarded as yet another test of the UK's European commitment. It was so regarded. And the UK Defence Secretary duly passed the test with his statement of intention to buy the A400M in May 2000.

The second, intelligence gathering, is very important indeed. With the shared Anglo-American interception and control of global information flows, their analysis and processing is a central feature of the Alliance. It is tightly held, not freely available to the NATO partners. Whether the existing arrangements with the United States could be sustained if GCHQ Cheltenham was brought within the proposed European Union intelligence service is far from certain. The European Union intelligence gathering facility would be based on the very costly developments of the French spy satellite Helios and in particular, the planned next generation, the Helios II.

A significant step in this direction was taken at the Franco-German

Summit in June 2000 when Chirac and Schroeder formally agreed to create a joint satellite reconnaissance system – overtly to make the European Union independent of American intelligence and outside of NATO.

This indeed is the creation of an *autonomous* European Union military capability. At the same meeting, the Germans also announced their decision to buy 75 air bus A400M military transport planes which, along with the orders made for the same military transport by Britain, France and Spain, could also be considered as a potential, additional, European Union autonomous capability – outside of NATO.

For the United Kingdom, the development of the European Union's Common Foreign Policy and its autonomous defence capacity to give it teeth has very serious and indeed threatening implications. What has been virtually ignored in public discussion so far is the principal anxieties that both the United States and British share: their wholly understandable misgivings about French policy and designs. In earlier chapters the development of an alternative French-led design for post-war Europe was documented and explored. That design developed significantly from the return to power of General de Gaulle in 1958 and was powerfully articulated by him in all the forums and associations where France was a member. For a variety of reasons, some highly individual to the General and others relating to his ambitions to restore France to the first rank of European and global powers, French policy in Europe concentrated on two clear objectives: one, to construct a partnership with Germany, with France as its senior member, and two, to deploy French influence and power to reduce and limit that of the United States in particular and of the Anglo-Saxons (including the United Kingdom) in general. High among the General's priorities was the deliberate repudiation of American ascendancy and leadership of NATO. De Gaulle's successors, Pompidou, Giscard d'Estaing, Mitterand and Chirac have been less abrasive than the General but none have dissented from the basic Gaullist strategy. The hostility to American power, the withdrawal of America from the European continent, its replacement by the forces of the European Union under Franco-German leadership is one of the realities of contemporary Europe. Nor is French opposition to American and British aims and interests confined to the European continent. In the Middle East, in the Israel/Arab conflict, in policy and sanctions against Iraq, in international trade policy and in agricultural trade in particular, French influence – and wherever possible, French-influenced European Union influence – is deployed *against* the United States

It is the knowledge of this, in both London and Washington, that inevitably leads to considerable anxiety about the new structures for defence and foreign policy now being developed by the European Union. For the United Kingdom, the conflict with France could not be clearer. Just as one of its most powerful and consistent strategic and foreign policy objectives since 1945 has been to keep America in Europe, so for France, to engineer the withdrawal of America from the continent has been a major strategic policy objective.

With the Cold War well behind us, it looks as though the French are winning the argument in the other capitals of Europe. Here, Germany is the key player. With its now reunited 80 million population and its powerful economy, Germany will inevitably play a very large part in the composition of any European Union military force. And Germany would play that part without arousing the anxieties in most other continental states that a strong separate German-controlled armed force would otherwise provoke. The importance that Germany's leaders attach to the Common Foreign Policy and the defence capability to give it strength was made clear by Chancellor Kohl just as soon as the Maastricht Treaty was signed when he said: 'A European army and European police force lie at the end of the road to European Union'.

This European-clothed ambition covers the whole spectrum of German politics as was shown a few years later in November 1998, on the eve of the new SPD government taking office, when Germany's new Foreign Minister Joschka Fischer said: 'Transforming the European Union into a single state with one army, one constitution, one foreign policy is the central challenge of the age'.

Once again the Franco-German Treaty has helped to ensure that the two most powerful of the continental states march in step in this, as in other crucial policy matters. In particular, ever since the Maastricht Treaty of 1992 and more clearly still in the Amsterdam Treaty of 1997, the project of European Common Defence and Foreign Policy has become a central issue, on the agenda of virtually all Heads of Government Council of Ministers' meetings. The German Presidency planned with the French in the months beforehand to advance substantially the defence project at the Cologne Summit in June 1999, and additionally the further advances made during the Finnish Presidency that followed, culminating in the Helsinki Heads of Government Council in December 1999. Developments have continued during the Portuguese Presidency in the first half of 2000 and the project will reach a culminating point during the French Presidency at the Nice Summit in December 2000.

Meanwhile supportive voices are speaking up in the different European institutions. The European Parliament is strongly, if predictably, in favour. Solana, the newly appointed High Representative, went so far as to come out publicly in support of an Italian proposal for a separate European Union seat on the United Nations Security Council while Signor Prodi, President of the Commission, has called for a new European Union Defence Treaty with the unambiguous purpose of giving 'us our own defence capabilities'.

The present Labour government in the United Kingdom, since the St Malo Summit, has been at first compliant in these developments and now, since Kosovo, openly enthusiastic for them.

But the long-term interests of the United Kingdom are a very different matter. First and foremost is the very real danger that the direction and thrust of the UK's foreign policy will increasingly be influenced by, and be subject to, the priorities and concerns of our Continental neighbours. They do not always coincide. The Continental countries are – understandably – Eurocentric. Everything that happens in Eastern Europe up to the Russian frontier and everything that happens in the Balkans are certainly of European Union concern. Additionally, the French colonial connections carry those interests into the Mahgreb and into Central Africa. If Turkey enters the European Union, part of the Middle East will also be within the area of direct concern.

Now that the Amsterdam Treaty is in force, and following the appointment of the energetic Mr Solana as the High Representative – or rather Foreign Secretary – of the European Union and Chris Patten as the Commissioner with the Foreign portfolio, the formation of a European Union common policy in these areas will be rapidly developed. The ten-page outline of the European Union's new common policy towards the Ukraine, as agreed at Helsinki and published in the Presidency's conclusions together with the earlier common policy statement on Russia and the still incomplete policy statement on the Mediterranean, are indications of what lies ahead.

Whether it is desirable at all that the European Union should form a common policy towards Russia, the Ukraine and the Mediterranean is itself a major question. It is true that that common strategies are, under the rules of the treaty, subject to veto if the United Kingdom or any other member state felt strongly enough so to object. But once agreed, measures to implement the common strategy, by joint actions and common positions, can thereafter under the treaty's rules be taken by qualified majority vote. If military actions were envisaged, the national veto again can be deployed. But the issue would need to be taken then by any dissenting state to a Heads of Government Council and reasons of national interest would have to be deployed to justify its resistance. In short, once a common strategy has been agreed, it will be a very difficult decision for any dissenting nation not to go along with the subsequent actions taken to enforce it. And even where the treaty rules are unambiguously clear that a veto right exists, it should never be forgotten that in the European Union, involvement in decision making is an endless series of bargains and trade-offs in which successful resistance to majority wishes in one area will almost certainly be accompanied by a concession somewhere else or the use of qualified majority voting powers to punish a dissenter.

So the first and most serious UK concern is the greatly increased pressure on the UK's foreign and defence policies to fall into line with the priorities and interests of the majority of European Union states. The second concern – that makes the first all the more serious – is the central fact that the UK's priorities and interests in external policy are larger than, and different from, those of its European Union partners. The Commonwealth connection and the UK involvement that this entails in events in Asia, Africa and Australasia – not to mention a score or more of islands, including the Falklands – has already been described. Nor can it be assumed that the interests of the European Union will not directly conflict with those of one or more Commonwealth countries. Those who follow these events will recall the clash between the rights of Canadian versus Spanish fishing boats in the North Atlantic when Spain, as a member of the European Union, was backed by Commissioner Bonino, the commissioner responsible for the Common Fisheries Policy, who decided that Spain's rights must be upheld by Community action, including the physical protection of Spanish fishing vessels. Fortunately the matter was settled. But not before the point had registered with serious British observers, of the possibility – however remote – of the Royal

Navy under European Command or direction having to threaten the protecting Canadian warships who belong to the Royal Canadian Navy.

Ludicrous of course. But a country whose government and whose law officers are prepared to fine and imprison those who sell fruit and vegetables in the shops and market stalls by imperial weights, rather than as instructed by the European Union in metric measures, cannot wholly be relied on.

The third and more practical point is that we have only limited resources in the FCO, the Ministry of Defence and in the Armed Forces. The UK has already committed several thousand troops in the earlier Bosnian peace-keeping operation and several thousand more in the dispatch of so-called K4 ground troops to Kosovo. Units of the RAF patrol the skies in the Iraqi no-fly zones in both the North and South of that country. In addition there are garrisons in Cyprus and the Falklands and the many battalions needed to fight terrorism in Northern Ireland. All these tasks require very substantial forces. Our ability to sustain them and to undertake further tasks is seriously limited. What could be made available elsewhere will be seriously reduced by the demands for a UK contribution to the sixty thousand 'rapid reaction' force, with supporting air and naval units as agreed at Helsinki for the new European Union Defence Force.

The reduction of force availability elsewhere and indeed the reduction of our diplomatic effort in the rest of the world are causes of genuine concern. The Cold War is over and, provided that NATO and the European Union are wise and restrained in developing their relationships with Russia and with the former Soviet states, now independent states, the danger of major conflict in Eastern Europe should, virtually, have vanished. But with Russia and some of her former Soviet Republics still possessing huge nuclear arsenals, as well as substantial conventional forces, it is much too early to dismantle the defence posture and basic force dispositions of NATO.

7. *The World Outside II*

Meanwhile as the events of the first post Cold War decade have shown, we can expect the outbreak of local and regional conflicts, a continuing temptation of the strong to attack the weak, the tensions and actual conflicts that can so easily arise where territories are in dispute or where a former unitary state breaks up due to its own internal stresses and contradictions. Mercifully, these conflicts fall well short of world war but there will inevitably be demands for responses from the international community when they arise in the future as they have done in the past.

The United Kingdom is not just a member of the United Nations, the organisation which we played so large a part in launching in 1945, we are a permanent member of its executive body, the Security Council, one of the Five who bear the major responsibility for maintaining world peace and for leading resistance to armed aggression. This is a role we are eminently suited to play. But we cannot perform it if our diplomacy is hobbled and constrained by collective decisions and pressures within the European Union: and we cannot perform it if our armed forces are already pre-committed to European tasks and under European defence structures.

What makes the present government's commitments in Cologne and Helsinki to the UK's participation in the new European defence force so remarkable is that throughout those months of negotiations a separate and parallel negotiation involving our armed forces was taking place between UK ministers and the UN, represented by Secretary General Mr Kofi Annan to designate and earmark UK armed forces for UN missions.

This is, on the face of it, an excellent project and one that was envisaged when the United Nations was set up in 1945. In essence, the agreement is to make available to the UN – if the Security Council agreed – previously designated armed forces which could, in an emergency, be rapidly deployed to carry out such tasks – including warfare – as the UN was authorised to undertake.

The Memorandum of Understanding signed in New York in June 1999 committed the United Kingdom to the deployment of designated ground, naval and air forces within a ten to thirty days' notification of their requirement. Since one of the UN's major difficulties in previous peace-keeping and peace-enforcement missions has been the unpreparedness and often slow force mobilisation of contributing member states, agreements in advance of trouble in the form of earmarked, stand-by forces are very desirable. Moreover, the Memorandum of Understanding is not a general, unquantified pledge to make forces available, but a detailed list, in its accompanying Annex, of helicopters, air transport and air defence units, of aircraft carriers, amphibious platforms, destroyers and frigates; of artillery, tanks and personnel carriers; of infantry battalions and other support units – a list of no less than seventy seven items, with specified ten-day or thirty-day availability.

The agreement with the UN was formally signed on 25 June 1999 – twenty one days after the Prime Minister, at the European Union's Cologne Summit, agreed the Declaration that committed the European Union to obtaining 'the capacity for autonomous action, backed up by credible military forces'. The French, it is true, made a similar commitment to the European Union and to the UN which, if seriously meant, would indeed be a departure in French post-war policy – and would raise similar questions about the size of their military forces and their ability to meet both the EU and UN commitments. Neither the UK nor France has even hinted at *increasing* their defence budgets. Remarkably, there has been little or no effort by Defence or Foreign Ministers to relate the commitments to each other and to the UK's existing military strength.

With defence expenditure down to 2.5 per cent of GDP, with the ludicrous assumption made by the Treasury of 3 per cent per annum 'efficiency savings', the UK is in serious danger of not being able to meet its current defence commitments, let alone additional ones.

Given the strength of the government's political commitment to Europe, to the Common Foreign Policy and the accompanying European Defence capability, the likelihood is that the UN and other commitments will be pushed very much into second place, and that both NATO and Anglo-American shared defence, intelligence, nuclear and other arrangements will be weakened.

Policies in the European Union and NATO are not yet firmly fixed. It is possible that the two-tier Europe that is now unavoidable (as argued in a previous chapter) could again accommodate different levels of integration and commitment. For example, the UK's contribution could be on a much-reduced scale; more important, the UK could insist that the so-called Petersburg Tasks exclude, without the positive assent of the House of Commons, the costly resource requirements of peace-making and peace-enforcement.

But for the UK the requirements of defence policy are clear. First, our own external defence, apart from what we ourselves directly contribute, is best secured (as is that of Europe as a whole) by NATO and not by any separate European Union military force. Second, it is in our interest to continue and to strengthen the special arrangements that we have with our principal ally, the United States. Third, that in any European Union force deployment, the UK should only take part if the decision is made with specific US agreement; and that the assets necessary to carry out the task should be those pre-designated from *within* NATO itself.

The Task Ahead

In our private lives, many of us, as a New Year approaches, briefly take stock of where we are and what we most desire for the year ahead. So it is with the nation's affairs. But on the eve of the year 2000, we had inevitably to reflect not just on the start of a new year, or even a new decade, but on a new century, even a new millennium.

Those latter timescales soar far beyond what anyone, without the gift of prophecy, can even begin to range. But at least the agenda of major problems that already confront us and which will undoubtedly be with us for several decades ahead can be stated and assessed. And it is with reference to that agenda that we can, hopefully, best decide what part in the early decades of this new century we, in Britain, can most usefully play.

First, there is the great question of international order, of war and peace, of how the 190 nation states can continue to live together, solve their problems and settle their disputes without resort to arms. And how we can best ensure that when one country does attack another the victim can be rescued, if need be by armed force to defeat the aggressor – not a new problem. As we have seen during the past half century, in Korea, in Kuwait and in East Timor, UN-sanctioned forces have been mobilised and successfully employed to defeat the aggressor or to rescue the victim.

But collective security and the renunciation of the use of force to settle disputes – the key doctrines enshrined in the Charter of the United Nations – are not available if one or other of the five permanent members of the United Nations Security Council – the USA, Russia, China, France and the UK – decides to use its veto power to prevent it. The five permanent members were of course the victorious allies who defeated Germany, Italy and Japan in the Second World War. Their power of veto was, at root, an acknowledgement of the realities of power: that to take military action against any of the Five would be costly and hazardous and could well lead, not to a limited exercise of collective security, but to major war of regional, even global, proportions. So, the Soviet Union was free to invade Hungary in 1956 and Czechoslovakia in 1968 – with only verbal protests in the United Nations. The United States, particularly in Latin America, acted both covertly and overtly against feared pro-Soviet regimes in Nicaragua, San Salvador, Chile – although it failed to topple Communism in Castro's Cuba. China was able to invade occupy and annex neighbouring Tibet. Only Britain and France, in their ill-judged joint attempt to seize the Suez Canal zone from Egypt, were obliged to desist and withdraw when the US and the USSR threatened action against them.

Looking ahead, although it would be unwise to ignore the continuing reality of great military power, the prospects look distinctly brighter. The Cold War, the global struggle between Soviet-led communism and the capitalist democracies is now over: and there seems to be virtually no serious prospect of its revival. The Soviet Union itself no longer exists and Russia and the fifteen countries of the Commonwealth of Independent States that have succeeded it have abandoned communism and embraced forms of elected government. Russia and a number of her neighbours are still unstable and there is a danger of a nationalist backlash in Russia itself.

But the West can do much to assist its former adversary and it is very much in its interest to secure democracy in that still very powerful country. As for the United States, as the undisputed leading superpower, the old Cold War interventionism has gone – along with the Cold War itself.

The only nation powerful enough to threaten regional, virtually global conflict and which is ruled by an ideologically radical and totalitarian elite is China. Its vast territory makes it the geographical neighbour of Russia, Mongolia and Kazakstan to the North; of Pakistan, Tajikistan and Kyrgyzstan to the West; of the Indian subcontinent, Burma and Vietnam to the South; of Korea and Japan to the East. To her geographical neighbours and indeed to countries further apart, China causes some considerable unease. Tibet is a continuing concern to India and it will be many years before Delhi forgets the short-lived invasion of Indian territory by Chinese troops in 1964. South Korea – and Japan – are rightly nervous both about Peking's support for the dangerous and maverick regime in North Korea and for the relentless build-up of Chinese military power, including nuclear weapons and long-range missiles. Most immediately threatening is of course China's claim to Taiwan and, behind that, the linked menace of a direct confrontation with the United States whose Seventh Fleet is the most tangible guarantee and long-term protection of an independent Taiwan.

None of this is cause for alarm and certainly not for despair. But finding a modus vivendi with China, with its 1,000 million plus people and its rapidly developing economy and industry, is the number one problem for those who hope for a world without major war in the twenty first century. China's economic pragmatism, its political skill in negotiating the 'one country, two systems' settlement with the former British colony of Hong Kong and the Portuguese colony of Macao, and its negotiated entry into the World Trade Organisation offer some grounds for optimism. And these must be reinforced by the prospects that, in an age of such ease of communication, the seeds of democracy blowing across China from the outside world will take root and grow and from within assist with the transformation of Chinese society and its system of government.

In the assimilation of China within the world economy and as a major player in the world political order, the principal actors must be the United States and the main geographical neighbours of China itself. The UK can only play a minor role, helped only by the insight and connections that two centuries of direct rule in Hong Kong have given us into Chinese society and politics and, beyond that, our instinctive support both for Tibet and its people and for their neighbour India to the South.

Provided only that the West and China can find the necessary accommodation, global conflict is now very unlikely. There remain, however, two lesser but still substantial problems – those posed by entrenched regional conflicts between powerful neighbours and the threats posed by a clutch of maverick, heavily-armed and unpredictable rogue states.

Of the regional conflicts, probably the most dangerous are the continued struggle of Israel with her Arab neighbours and of India with Pakistan, particularly over Kashmir. These conflicts involve conflicting perceptions of national security, of rights to territory and self-government, but they are also deepened by opposing religious faiths and fundamentalism.

Both disputes have remained unresolved for more than fifty years. Serious armed clashes have occurred between India and Pakistan on no less than three occasions and four wars – all-out wars, though short-lived – have been fought between Israel and her Arab neighbours. None of these conflicts has been decisive and hostility between the nations concerned has been kept alive by continuing guerrilla and terrorist actions.

The solution to these long-standing conflicts is made all the more urgent by the open acquisition by both Pakistan and India of nuclear weapons – and missile delivery systems. Israel too has a nuclear weapon capability and among her most determined enemies both Iraq and Iran have long-range missiles and are developing nuclear weapon programmes – although in the case of Iraq, both missiles and nuclear developments have been halted since 1991 – until a year ago – by the activities of the UN arms inspectors, located in Iraq itself.

In both conflicts an extra dimension of bitterness is provided by religious extremism. In Israel, Hebrew fanaticism is fortunately confined to a relatively small minority. But it does have a stronger presence in Jerusalem and the Jewish settlements around that city than anywhere else – the place where, within the general problem of the Arab/Israeli conflict, future control poses a uniquely difficult problem. Moreover, while religious fanaticism effects only a minority, the Israeli Proportional Representation (PR) system of election often gives a handful of extremist MPs a decisive influence in the Knesset. On the Arab side, a major factor in the whole approach, not only of the Palestinians in the West Bank, the Gaza Strip and in the refugee camps elsewhere but in the politics of a number of their Arab League protectors, is Islamic fundamentalism. However distorted their interpretation of the Koran and Muslim teaching may be, hatred of the 'Infidel' provides justification for Hezbollah and other terrorist organisations not only for continuing acts of terrorism but also for the open advocacy of tyranny at home and Jihad abroad.

The conflict between India and Pakistan is more secular than religious. But Pakistan's *raison d'être* as a state is its overwhelmingly Muslim population and its self-definition as an Islamic state. India is a secular democracy but continuing conflict with Pakistan over Kashmir has helped to strengthen Hinduism to the point where, in the mid-1990s for the first time since independence, the Hindu Jatiya Party (BJP) became the majority party in the Indian government coalition.

What now are the prospects ahead? Very substantial efforts have been made and continue to be made to find a settlement in the Middle East. The peace process, launched and developed so secretly and so helpfully in Oslo, has made only slow progress – and at times has been brought to a halt. But progress *has* been made, Israeli governments are committed to the peace process and so are Arafat and the Palestinian leadership. Egypt and Jordan are clearly supportive as, less prominently, are Saudi Arabia and the Gulf States. Only Iran (fortunately at the far edge of the Arab world) and Iraq (neutralised by its defeat in the Kuwait war) remain totally hostile, while Syria has moved – however slightly – from its previously hard-line rejectionist stance.

Two additional factors give strong reasons for at least a guarded optimism. One of course is the end of the Cold War and to the deliberate enflaming of hostility by the Soviet supply of weapons and propaganda to the hard-line Arab states. The second factor is the continued generous support, in both diplomacy and economic assistance, of the United States, not only for Israel from the very inception of that state in 1947 but in more recent years for Egypt and the PLO.

It would be wrong to overstate the UK's influence in the area and in furthering the peace process there. But we do enjoy and have enjoyed the confidence and friendship of successive Israeli governments, in spite of the Foreign Office tilt in favour of the Arab world – where we certainly have strong contacts, political and economic, in particular with the Kingdom of Jordan and the Gulf states. Once again, the objectives of a peaceful solution, combining security for Israel with the right to self-determination of the Palestinian people and of promoting the cause of democracy in the Middle East, make us a strong supporter of American efforts in this area. And here too it is necessary to note that while the influence of the European Union has been small, France in particular has played a far from supportive role – motivated by both the desire to increase its own exports to the rich countries of the region and to challenge and reduce American – and British – interests there.

And what of the Indian subcontinent? Some new initiatives are urgently needed. Pakistan becomes politically more unstable, with its frequent changes of government, some elected, some imposed either directly by the army or by the exercise of Presidential power. Among the former Prime Ministers of Pakistan in the past twenty five years, one, Mr Bhutto was hanged, another his daughter Benazir, is in exile and the third, Mr Sharif, is in prison, found guilty of the attempted murder of General Musharaff, now the acting head of state. The whole country has been flooded with weapons acquired from the Afghans, so abundantly supplied by the United States in the early 1990s to all opponents of the then Soviet-imposed Communist regime in Kabul. Shia and Sunni wage intermittent war on each other and breakaway movements, in the Sind, Baluchistan and the Punjab grow in strength. Corruption is rife throughout the public services and every level of government. The temptations of the Pakistan military to intervene, to 'clean up' the government and restore civil order at home and to win some popular support by aggressive words against neighbouring India and through the supply of weapons, training and bases for the pro-Pakistan forces in Kashmir, are great indeed. India, for its part is less affected by internal pressures and less prone to rash and provocative actions: but Kashmir poses for India a fundamental problem because it affects the legitimacy of a large number of territories within the State of India itself. The grant of independence to Kashmir, let alone its association with Pakistan, would have very threatening repercussion in other parts of India where Muslim majorities exist and where accession to the Union in 1947 was secured only by princely choice.

In this very serious dispute, the UK is inescapably if indirectly involved. It is a seriously divisive issue in some parts of the UK where large numbers of subcontinent immigrants from Kashmir itself and from its neighbouring provinces in both India and Pakistan have settled and brought the issues and the conflict with them. As the former imperial power and the joint author, along with the Indian Congress and the Muslim League of the whole partition settlement in 1947, our past responsibility and involvement are self-evident. Since the withdrawal of the Raj, British diplomacy in the subcontinent has always been directed to reducing the hostility between the two main states – and maintaining influence and goodwill with both. It has not been an easy assignment. As Foreign Secretary Robin Cook discovered when accompanying the Queen on her fiftieth Anniversary of Independence visit in 1997, infelicitous statements and clumsy offers of mediation, well-intentioned as they may have been, can easily lead to offended irritability and are counterproductive.

This is a problem where Britain in the Commonwealth rather than the UK acting on its own can be most effective. In the first instance it would be of great help for the Commonwealth Secretariat to take private soundings of some of the neighbouring states – Bangladesh, Sri Lanka, Nepal and those other Commonwealth states that are known to have particularly close connections with either Pakistan or India – and then, in the light of those soundings, to make discreet approaches to both countries.

Pakistan of course is already on the Commonwealth Agenda, following the Durban CHOGM in December 1999 with demands on Pakistan for the restoration of democratic government. The fact that the subcontinent is one of the few areas of the globe where American power has played and continues to play – in spite of President Clinton's late-in-the-day personal visit – only a minor role, makes Commonwealth and UK involvement all the more important. The European Union could perhaps also assist: but there is no serious interest or involvement by our European associates in the subcontinent's affairs.

Both the Middle East and India/Pakistan pose difficult and dangerous problems. But here too there are grounds for optimism. Without minimising the destabilising effects of the fanatics' favourite weapon, the bomb, ours is an age where governments and peoples are becoming increasingly aware both of the tactics of terrorism and the ideologies, religious and secular, which motivate them; and, increasingly, governments refuse to be provoked into that outraged matching violence on which the terrorist relies. Moreover in most parts of the globe totalitarian parties of both right and left have ceased to command majorities, secularism has subdued religious fanaticism and elected representative government has become the norm.

Indeed it is the absence of these moderating influences, the survival of totalitarian-type government coupled with the possession of advanced weapon technology that makes a few, mainly isolated, rogue states such a threat to peace and security in the period ahead. Iraq under Saddam Hussein, with his murderous instincts and possession of advanced military technology and weapons of mass destruction, is a real and continuing threat to the peace of the whole Middle East region. Similarly, the ideologically near-insane government of North Korea with its arsenal of nuclear weapons and its long-range missiles can directly threaten vast areas of East and South Asia and supply rocket launchers to whoever will buy them, including that friend and sponsor of terrorism Gaddafi in Libya. In the future, weapons of mass destruction will become increasingly easy to acquire and the problem that they pose will not be solved just by treaties and conventions, renouncing biological, chemical and nuclear weapons. For the most part, the rogue states will not even bother to sign them.

So what is to be done? The maintenance of international peace and security requires effective preventative action. It cannot simply wait for a rogue state to break international law by itself attacking a neighbour. Such action could well be adopted by, and channelled through, existing UN machinery. Chapter VII of the Charter empowers the Security Council of the UN to deal not only with breaches of the peace and acts of aggression but with 'threats to the peace'. It is of course possible for one of the Permanent Five to veto a programme of compulsory weapon-of-mass-destruction inspection or an economic blockade of materials needed for a weapons programme but, with the possible exception of China protecting North Korea, it is highly unlikely that any other permanent member would risk the odium of such action. This is an initiative that Britain could well undertake and with a great deal of support from its many partners – in the United States, the EU and the Commonwealth. Such an initiative could of course flop but it seems to be more likely to attract support and actually contribute to world peace and security than the empty posturing of Robin Cook's ethical foreign policy.

The last item on the peace-war-security agenda of our new century could well become the most dangerous and difficult of them all: the waging of the 'just war' in the pursuit and global enforcement of human rights. Over the past several decades, human rights have received growing attention everywhere and most certainly in democratic states. The UN has of course its own Committee on Human Rights but the main developments have been in Europe. With the hideous abuses of Nazi Germany still very much in mind, almost the first act of the newly-established Council of Europe in 1950 was to set up the European Court of Human Rights, with its panel of judges drawn from different signatory countries, and a complaints machinery, to rule on disputed matters affecting the human rights of citizens in the member states, even when they had exhausted the whole judicial and appeal machinery of their own countries. The main thrust behind this was of course to provide an avenue for protest, to an impartial and authoritative body, with high status and high publicity, against some future state tyranny that might crush internal political and judicial rights – as had happened in so many European countries in the 1920s and 30s.

Moreover, in the mid-1970s the Helsinki Accords, which were reached during a period of *détente* with the USSR, contained Human rights provisions whereby it was accepted by the Soviet Union and the other Communist governments in Eastern Europe that alleged abuses of human rights in all signatory countries could be legitimately raised and investigated.

Most recently, the European Union in the 1997 Amsterdam Treaty and most notably in the Tampere Heads of Government Council in October 1999 proclaimed itself to be an area of freedom and justice, extended its non-discrimination and its citizens rights programmes and with it the competence of its own European Court of Justice, and embarked upon drafting an ambitious Charter of Fundamental Human Rights. With all these go of course not just moral obligations but also public indictment and punitive fines against those found guilty of offence.

Even within the European Union there are very serious and worrying implications of the increasing rule by unelected judges, not in great matters of unmasking political tyranny and defending democracy, but in its growing extension into every area of social conduct and national life where previously elected governments and Parliaments had prevailed.

But the biggest problem that has emerged is the new doctrine of Human Rights promotion and enforcement in other sovereign states. The 1999 war over Kosovo, part of the sovereign state of Serbia, carried the human rights doctrine far beyond all previous limits, when the NATO alliance waged war on Serbia for what the allies considered to be unacceptable violations of human rights, particularly the ethnic cleansing of the Albanian minority in Kosovo. There are indeed many most important issues yet to be fully explored and settled in the whole Kosovo operation – including the lack of *formal* UN legitimisation and sanction for the military operation there.

But, whatever retrospective analysis and judgement may be reached, what is clear is that a substantial part of the world community was ready to support action against a sovereign state, not for attacking a neighbouring state, which is clearly forbidden by the UN Charter, but for what other countries judged to be gross misconduct and abuse of human rights *within* its own territory This does indeed raise novel and most serious issues.

The implications of the Kosovo war can of course be partly limited by the fact that the Serb action inevitably turned an internal matter into an external one by the sheer scale of the flight or expulsion of Albanian Kosovars across the borders into neighbouring Macedonia and Albania, with most serious destabilising consequences for those two small countries.

But that in itself imposes only a small restraint on future action. The truth is, that without the most carefully considered and imposed new rules of conduct, the pursuit of human rights by the use of armed force can open up a new era of instability in world affairs that could destroy the prospect of lasting peace in the twenty first century.

In the espousal and pursuit of human rights, it has to be recognised that genuine humanitarian concern can all too easily provide a cloak for other less worthy pursuits connected with national and group advantage, not to mention the personal goals and ambitions of political leaders. Further, where that concern for the suffering and abuse of fellow human beings is fed and sometimes actively promoted by the mass media and above all by television's emotive pictures of the dead, the wounded, the tearful children and the columns of refugees, the 'something must be done' demand for action in a democracy can become almost irresistible.

Yet, all around the world, history has left its legacy of cultural, religious or ethnic minorities living in countries where the majority community holds the reins of power. In well established democracies, that problem exists but is normally greatly eased, if never wholly removed, by accommodation and recognition of minority rights.

In many parts of the world, not excluding the Western democracies themselves, but most notably in countries which have only recently achieved self-government and where forms of elected government following years of authoritarian rule, are still rather

213

precariously established, there is a clear danger that external pressures for human rights in general and ethnic rights in particular will lead to the escalation of impractical and irresponsible minority demands. Worse, it can positively encourage extremist groups to assertive action, including the right to secede, backed-up with every means of pressure including terrorism that threaten the state itself with disintegration and chaos.

Finally, if the cause of gross violation of human rights is the existence of an authoritarian government or a still unemptied store of majority/minority hatred, external armed intervention to defend human rights is likely to lead only to an increase in the original hatred or the need to create, *de facto* or *de lege*, a separate state, under the semi-permanent armed guard of its outside protectors.

In his Chicago speech, delivered on 22 April 1999, in the middle of the Kosovo crisis, Prime Minister Tony Blair attempted to define a doctrine of human rights intervention which would in the future help us to 'decide when and whether to intervene' and did lay down some limitations on obedience to what would otherwise be the endless demands of the moral imperative. But there are several more searching questions that need an answer before we can begin to define the boundaries of what actions are acceptable. First among them is whether or not the doctrine of human rights armed intervention is a doctrine that applies only to Europe – or rather that part which lies West of the Polish-Romanian borders. Or is it a doctrine that can embrace territories to the East, to Chechnya in Russia, to Azerbaijan, to Armenia and Georgia as well? And if it can apply to geographical Europe up to the Caucasus, can it not also apply to the Indian subcontinent, to Kashmir, to the Congo and Rwanda and indeed anywhere else where significant minority populations seek rights for themselves that their governments are not prepared to allow or where separatist movements demand their own statehood?

One has only to pose the questions to conclude that human rights interventionism, in its military form, has only the most limited application. That does not exclude other forms of pressure, diplomatic and economic, that external powers can bring to bear upon those states that unacceptably abuse the human rights of their own people.

Is there not another, perhaps, better way to proceed? Has not the international community reached the point where, having breached the UN Charter's own Article 2 (7) which forbids intervention in matters which 'are essentially within the domestic jurisdiction of any state', it should take the path not just of pursuing human rights as the immediate goal but of *promoting democracy* as the only means of providing long-term solutions to the violation of group and individual rights. For the advocates of human rights, democracy provides two immensely important safeguards: first: the elected representation of minority communities in the assembly/parliament of the country concerned and second, because democracy can only operate with free elections and open debate, the articulation of grievance – and the support of the aggrieved – become part and parcel of the electoral process. Further, the accommodations that are necessary, the rights that need to be established, are far more secure when achieved by the processes of internal debate, pressure and legislation than when they are enforced by external sanction and armed power. Here again is an approach and a cause particularly suited to the United Kingdom – and to its partners both in the post-Harare Commonwealth and in NATO.

All these direct threats to peace and security, the dangers of armed conflict that they pose are of course only the most visible and the most immediate of the many equally, if not more important, problems that crowd the agenda of our new century.

Top of any list of the non-military threats to our security is the question of how to maintain and improve the health and strength of the world economy. The last half of the twentieth century was for the economically-developed nations of Western Europe, North America,

Japan and Australasia – all the member states of the Organisation for Economic Co-operation and Development, the OECD – a period not only of peace but of unparalleled growth in national wealth and improved living standards. The key question is: can we sustain it in the decades ahead, in a period of still accelerating change? And can we bring into this charmed circle of prosperity the great bulk of mankind that lives in economically undeveloped countries, including the hundreds of millions who still dwell in abject poverty.

To take first the advanced countries: within that general aim of sustainable growth and rising living standards, can we achieve three subsidiary but supporting objectives: that we sustain a high level of employment; that trade between the main trading nations remains open and that global economic management is successful in sufficiently regulating the boom-to-slump cyclical tendencies of market capitalism in order to avoid major recessions? In the history of the last century the Great Slump that followed the Wall Street crash of 1929 was a key factor that led to mass unemployment and falling living standards throughout the developed world; to trade wars and protectionism between the major economic powers; to the growth of extremist, totalitarian parties of both left and right and to the overthrow of democracy in Germany and its replacement by the dictatorship of the Nazi party.

In the second half of that century, the West has avoided anything approaching that catastrophe. But on at least two occasions the world has had a glimpse of the chaos and damage that economic events can still inflict: first, the oil crisis of 1973 with its temporary interception of oil supplies to the West and the long-term quadrupling of oil prices that immediately ensued; second, the 1998-9 financial collapse of the banking and credit systems of the so-called 'tiger' economies of South East Asia, rapidly communicating to Russia and Latin America and nearly toppling the currency and banking system of Brazil.

216

8. The Task Ahead

Fortunately the co-operation established between the oil-consuming countries and the non-OPEC oil-producing states in 1973 and, in the late 1990s, the active intervention of the IMF to bring about more realistic exchange rates and financial disciplines in the over-borrowed and over-heated 'tiger' economies, were able to turn the tide.

But few observers of the world scene, particularly in the financial crisis of the late 1990s, could fail to recognise the absolutely key role played by the United States in making available additional credit facilities either directly or through the IMF to the 'tiger' economies and, above all, by acting as an 'importer of last resort', willing and able to absorb the vast export surge from the 'tiger' economies and the developing world where internal domestic markets had virtually collapsed.

The willingness and ability of the United States to play this leading role of guarantor of the world economy along with its partners in the Group of Seven, was essential to avoid an economic collapse, with political repercussions that can only be guessed at. What cannot be overlooked was the total failure of the European Union to play any part in helping to solve the crisis. Caught up and preoccupied in the last phases of launching the single currency, the Euro, the Commission and the major countries – Germany, France, Italy, Spain and Holland – were pursuing policies designed to *reduce* internal demand in the effort to achieve, above all other things, its own self-imposed goal of holding down the rate of inflation. And in an economic environment that was essentially deflationary for industry and farming. Virtually oblivious to the world outside, the central aim of macro-economic policy was to *cut* 'excess borrowing' by either reducing public expenditure or by raising taxation. Looking ahead, there must be a serious doubt as to the ability of the European Union, saddled as it is with its monetarist doctrines and obsessions with inflation which are, unfortunately, embedded in the clauses of the Maastricht Treaty itself, to make any worthwhile contribution to solving similar crises in the world economy that may arise in the future.

217

The same obsessions – and related disregard for the level of domestic unemployment – have the wider, political danger, if unemployment continues at its present high levels, of alienation and instability affecting the political order, democracy itself. For the past decade, with its 18 million unemployed, 10 per cent of its labour force, the European Union has ceased to be an area of high growth and low unemployment. And with this, there is a growing danger that the demand for protectionist measures will spread from the agricultural sector to goods and services in the effort to preserve jobs at home by keeping out the more competitive, low-priced exports of both the United States and the developing world.

These developments are of course directly relevant to the great question of opening up still further the markets of the developed nations to the products not just of the 'tiger' economies but to the much larger and now fast-developing countries of Asia and Latin America. China first but India not far behind, are bound as they develop to alter profoundly the size, shape and structure of world trade and the development of the internet's pricing transparency, which is itself deflationary, will force more production to low cost countries in the developing world.

The World Trade Organisation, the successor body to GATT, has at least provided a framework of basic rules and arbitration procedures for the regulation of world trade. But huge problems – as the abortive Seattle Conference of late 1999 so clearly revealed – have yet to be solved before agreements can be reached on such key questions as unfair competition, including cheap labour and child labour, environmental damage, tax and direct subsidies.

No country is better placed to articulate the needs of the developing world to the governments of the affluent West than the United Kingdom – through its close and intimate contacts with a range of developing nations. Certainly at Seattle the UK delegation was in close touch with the Commonwealth countries represented there. But the plain truth is that, under the European Union arrangements, we no longer have a voice even in the forum of the WTO. Asked directly the question who spoke for Britain, the Secretary of State for Trade and Industry or the European Commissioner Mr Lamy, the Minister of State replied on 10 December 1999: 'My Rt Hon Friend the Secretary of State for Trade and Industry speaks for the United Kingdom in the formation of European Union policy which Commissioner Lamy then represents in the World Trade Organisation'.

Yes: but it isn't just the European Union countries who should hear what the United Kingdom has to say but also representatives of the world's other 130 nations represented in the WTO.

The value of an independent and articulate UK voice in these matters was demonstrated in the negotiation and adoption of the Montreal Protocol to the UN Convention on Bio-Safety at the end of January 2000, when after five years of talks, Ministers agreed to a set of rules governing the highly controversial trade in living modified organisms (LMOs) created by modern biotechnology. One of the most controversial matters that had previously divided nations in the World Trade Organisation was thus removed, with the WTO accepting that the existing rule that trade in genetically modified organisms could only be halted where there was 'sufficient scientific evidence' to justify restraint, was replaced by the 'precautionary principle' which permits trade restriction or prohibition before scientific evidence can be mobilised to prove the dangers of serious environmental/health damage. This however remains a very difficult and contentious area of dispute in world trade. A distinction has to be drawn between national defences against the import of *potentially* dangerous – and actually harmful – genetically modified products and the *misuse* of these concerns to justify what are in fact protectionist measures in the interest of high-cost domestic farmers. Again, the UK is well placed to understand both sides of the argument: the European Union, with its highly protected large-scale farming industry is constantly tempted to use and exploit consumer food safety and environment worrying groups to argue the protectionist case while the UK, again with its special position in the Commonwealth and its closeness to the United States and its own rapidly expanding biotechnology industry, has close connections with the so-called Miami Group which includes, apart from Canada and the United States, Australia, Argentina, Uruguay and Chile, the main low-cost and innovative food producers.

The biggest problems of all, however, are those associated with continuing growth of the world's population, the vast numbers who live in poverty in different parts of the world and the determination of so many, previously economically stagnating countries to modernise and claim their share of world resources and prosperity.

This twenty first century opens with the world population of 6 billion as against a known total of 2.5 billion only fifty years earlier. Of today's total, roughly a third are the peoples of China and India and roughly one half inhabit the Asian mainland and its island chains. And of this total, something like 800 million are below the minimally accepted poverty line. The Asian 'tiger' economies, including South Korea, Indonesia, Malaysia, Singapore, Taiwan, the Philippines and Thailand account for some 300 millions – or only 10 per cent of the population of Asia. Their impact however, as with that of Japan in the 1960 to 1985 period, has been profound – not merely in providing a spectacular increase in their own living standards but also in achieving a strong presence in the industries and markets of the West. To mention but a few, shipbuilding, steel, electronics, motor cars, telecommunications and computers are industries where South Korea, Taiwan and Japan have a strong international presence.

Yet, to re-emphasise the point, these 'tiger' economies plus Japan account for less than 15 per cent of the population of the Asian countries. What we have to accept and come to terms with is that in the half-century ahead the near certainty is that the transformation from predominantly developing to developed economies will take place in virtually the whole of Asia and in particular in China and India.

8. The Task Ahead

Fortunately, trade and economic development need not be a zero sum game. Asian prosperity – and of course that of Latin America and more problematically Africa too – will provide not only a challenge to the West's own markets but new opportunities in those vastly expanded markets as well. All this will require a very substantial development of global economic management. United Nations specialised agencies, the IMF and the World Bank and the informal Group of Seven (plus Russia) are well established, but there is a clear need for a redefinition and expansion of their roles in the global economy. Again, the UK has a particular role to play with its unrivalled links to the United States, the European Union and the Commonwealth.

Today, the essential message that has to be signalled to the developing world from the advanced economies of the West is that there *is* room for all; that we *believe* in open markets and shared prosperity; that we understand that not all countries can accept exactly the same rules and obligations, at exactly the same time; and that all countries and their inhabitants, rich and poor alike, face limitations and constraints that together they must seek to resolve – the danger of pollution; the danger of disease (of which Aids, malaria and tuberculosis are simply the most prominent; the danger of exhaustion of raw materials, water supplies, oil, gas and other energy supplies). All possess the potential for conflict, division and worse, unless human intelligence and goodwill are mobilised to solve them.

It is in this world, the world of the present and the foreseeable future, that we must locate ourselves and our island and decide how best we can contribute to our own security and welfare, to that of our close neighbours across the Channel, to our still closer sister nations Australia, Canada and New Zealand, to our partners and close friends in the Commonwealth, to the 'cousins' in America who speak our language and share so many of our values and concerns.

One thing is quite clear. Our future cannot lie in immersing ourselves into the European State that, sooner or later, will emerge in at least Western Europe. We are indeed, as General de Gaulle so accurately defined us, 'maritime' as well as insular, genuinely global in our connections. So we can be only partly in Europe – never at its centre.

We are destined for something else, a multi-role future. There is an irony in this. Post-war Britain, as defined by its great war leader Winston Churchill and without hesitation adopted by both his successors as Prime Minister, Attlee and Eden, was unique in that we were positioned by history as well as geography at the intersection of three concentric circles: the first was the Commonwealth and Empire, the second was the English-speaking world and the third was Europe.

This self-evidently correct perspective of the UK was of course from 1960 onwards scorned as fantasy, romanticism, self deception, and over-weaning pride by successive generations of Europhile journalists, such as contemporaries Hugo Young and Andrew Marr, by retired diplomats, contemporary historians and media pundits. It was not only scorned and reviled but attacked as a dangerous and misleading perception, diverting the national gaze from its true target and focus: unity with Europe.

Yet the conception of concentric circles with the UK playing a significant part in each is today no more than the recognition of reality. We *are* a member of the European Union and as long as we are there we cannot fail to play a significant part within it; we *are* a leading member of that strangely enduring, increasingly significant, Commonwealth of more than fifty nations, located in every continent in the globe; we *do* have a special ease and alliance and friendship with the English-speaking nations and the US; we *are*, with our position as a permanent member of the Security Council of the United Nations, a significant player in the world community.

It is in our own interests – and that of our associates – that we continue in all these groupings and arrangements and are free to speak and act in each of them, within the limits of our resources, and as we see fit in the service of those causes of peace, resistance to aggression, democracy and the rule of law that engage all that is finest in the past and present of the British people.

Seven Conclusions

To tell the story of Britain's evolving relationships with her continental neighbours – and hopefully, to make that account intelligible – I have found it necessary to cover more than half-a-century's history of events. This has not been confined to just Britain and the European Community but has had to include major events in the other five continents in whose affairs the United Kingdom is also involved.

In the second part of this book, I have attempted to describe our existing options, both within the European Union and with our partners in the Commonwealth, and with our friends and allies in the United States and elsewhere. With a due sense of humility, I have also tried to discern in the decades that lie immediately ahead those problems that could threaten our own and our allies' peace and security, together with the most obvious problems that will face us as we seek both to maintain our own prosperity and to see that far more of it is shared with the rest of mankind than hitherto.

What conclusions are we entitled to draw? Some have already been stated in the different chapters devoted to major specific issues, such as the single currency and defence commitments. But a number have been left implicit, or only half explicit – and certainly they are scattered around the text. It may help therefore to draw them together here, and summarise briefly, what those conclusions are – together with the global institutional framework best suited to meet our existing and emerging needs.

I have seven major findings. *First*, on the relationship with the EU.

Nearly thirty years of membership have demonstrated the essential truth about Britain and its continental neighbours: we are good friends and allies and happy to co-operate in many joint endeavours. But the British people simply do not share the widespread desire, among the governments and peoples of their neighbouring European states, to develop an 'ever-closer union' to the point where national decision making has been largely replaced by either majority votes in the Council of Ministers or by supranational authorities in Europe. These include the unelected European Central Bank, the unelected Brussels Commission, the unelected European Court of Justice and the elected, but impotent, European Parliament. We did not experience, during those traumatic years of the Second World War, that common destiny of defeat, ruin, occupation and liberation that our continental neighbours were forced to endure. The curious bonding that arose from that shared humiliation and defeat was an experience that we could not and did not share. Nor have we endured the experience, repeated more than once since 1870, of German conquest or invasion of its neighbours – that scarring experience that has inspired successive French governments to construct an ever stronger constitutional cage to contain their over-powerful neighbour.

In all this, our approach has been shaped neither by prejudice nor by ignorance nor by old hatreds; we have simply reflected our island geography and the separate history that that geography, particularly the Channel and the Atlantic – the sheltering seas – have enabled us to shape.

Second – and linked closely to the first – we conspicuously lack any strong sense of European identity. In recent years, there has been much discussion about identity and, in particular, whether the sense of identity within Britain itself is strong enough to continue to keep subordinate the parallel sense of identity that people in geographical England, Wales, Scotland and Northern Ireland undoubtedly feel.

I think it is. But the crucial point is that *unless* such a strong identity continues to exist, there can be no possibility of maintaining long-term our commonly accepted sovereignty.

Clearly, that strong and necessary sense of identity does not exist between Britain and Europe. The evidence for this statement is overwhelming. Some five years ago, to mark the twentieth anniversary of Britain's 1975 referendum, the BBC asked the Mori-poll to report on the British people's attitudes to Europe.

A substantial sample of 2,000 electors were asked these most salient questions: first, how European do you feel; and second with which of a list of six countries (France, Germany, Spain and the United States, Canada and Australia) do you feel you have most in common?

The conclusions – and there was virtually no difference between the figures for different age groups – made quite plain that the bond of sentiment, of a special relationship or of identity with our main European Union neighbours was weak indeed. To the first question, how European do you feel etc., 8 per cent said a 'great deal' and 15 per cent a 'fair amount' while 49 per cent said: 'not at all'. And on the countries with whom people felt they had 'most in common', 9 per cent said France, 7 per cent Germany and 5 per cent Spain. In contrast, for the English-speaking countries, the figures were 23 per cent for the United States, 15 per cent Australia and 14 per cent Canada. In short, while 21 per cent felt they had 'most in common' with three of our principal European neighbours, no less than 52 per cent chose the three English-speaking nations, separated as they are by several thousand miles of ocean from the United Kingdom.

The European Union, through the Information Department of the Brussels Commission, itself polls opinion in the member states. Every six months, the europoll records the state of feeling towards the European Community-European Union of the peoples of its now 15 member states. And year after year, poll after poll, places the United Kingdom as the least enthusiastic, the least committed of them.

The British people cannot be frog-marched to the altar, a pistol at their heads, and told to take out the vows of eternal love and commitment to a European bride for whom they have only friendly feelings.

My *third* conclusion follows, inexorably, from the above: from the gulf that separates European aspirations from British realities. British governments, Labour or Tory, one after another, are forced to live a kind of lie about their relationships with Europe. They tell our European partners that Britain wishes to be 'at the heart of Europe'. But they tell the British people that the European Union is only about co-operating with neighbour states to do things more effectively than we can do on our own. Doubletalk, deception and self-deception do not make for healthy politics or honest debate. But there is a further and potentially much more damaging consequence for our democracy. In signing up to successive European Treaties, with their very special supranational features, we are entering into commitments that allow the European institutions to make, more and more, the laws in our land – without the specific consent of our electors or our Parliament. Inevitably, such laws lack the legitimacy of consent and sooner or later will lead those adversely affected to open defiance or worse. As it is, governments are constantly engaged in the task of hiding from the British people the fact that unpopular decisions are being made not by the Westminster Parliament but by one or other of the unelected bodies in Europe. For those who respect, with all their imperfections, our democracy and our Westminster Parliament, this is an intolerable situation – and it is one that is bound to get worse.

The *fourth* major conclusion of this study is that there is really no limit, no frontier, to the encroachment of European institutions on our national affairs. While the public gaze, understandably, has been focused on the crucial issue of the pound and the single currency, the European integrationists have made a substantial and dangerous inroad into the control of our own foreign and defence policies. Unless it is halted, the European Union's present drive to establish a common European foreign and defence policy will increasingly absorb and engulf the UK's own foreign policy. The control over our own foreign policy – including our ability to articulate the issues and causes we support, to use our resources to disadvantage enemies and reward friends and to determine our own defence and security arrangements – is essential to our continued independence as a sovereign state.

These European initiatives in foreign and defence matters are relatively new developments. The country has not yet begun to understand what is taking place. It is a process that the Blair government has not just accepted but actively encouraged – and it will make a fundamental change in the very nature of the European Union. What has been primarily an economic and social Union is now being developed into a quasi state, with its own foreign policy and a military capacity to project European power outside its own frontiers.

The priorities of our continental neighbours are not necessarily the same as our own. The UK has not just a European role – which it played to the full in the difficult years of the Cold War – but it has connections and responsibilities elsewhere and a role to play as a permanent member of the Security Council of the United Nations. It cannot play those roles if its armed forces are virtually absorbed within the 'rapid reaction' forces and command structures of the European Union and made available for their priority use.

Moreover with every further advance towards European Union, the voice and vote of a member state becomes absorbed within the European Union. I do not believe, that for Britain to have a voice in formulating the European Union's external policies and then accepting that the European Union (whether in the person of the Commissioner for External Affairs or the new High Representative of the European Council) thereafter is empowered to speak for

228

Britain, is an adequate exchange for the loss of the right to speak and vote in the wider councils of the world.

My *fifth* conclusion follows logically from the first four. We need to establish a new treaty relationship with the European Union, one that recognises and accepts the differences of purpose and history that separate the UK from many of its European neighbours, one which accepts a necessary repatriation of powers from the institutions of the Union to the UK.

This will not be easy. But past experience shows that it is far from impossible to arrange a UK exemption from new European Union laws, directives, judgements etc: all that is required now is agreement on an opt-out protocol for the UK from *all* future treaties and, domestically, an amendment to the 1972 European Communities Act under which for any future European Union enactment to be effective, it will need to have the authority of an affirmative order in the UK Parliament.

However, to sift through the accumulated laws and treaty commitments already entered into, to agree what needs to be discarded and what powers should be repatriated to the UK – and over a realistic time scale – is much more difficult, perhaps impossible. But it is a task worth essaying.

It is worth pursuing because, as already explained, a virtually unique opportunity for such change has arisen. There is the Helsinki commitment by the European Union states – as recent as December 1999 – to admit a further twelve applicant members. They will bring with them problems of such a magnitude and require such major adjustments of existing EU policies that accommodation within a single treaty is virtually impossible. A two-speed, or multi-speed Europe is not enough. A two-tier or multi-tier Europe is inevitable. And their entry almost certainly rules out any possibility of achieving with all twenty seven participating members that still deeper integration that the Founding Six and their closest allies are urgently seeking.

The French government for one has clearly woken up to the implications. In an interview with the newspaper *La Croix* on 3 April 2000, M Pierre Moscovici, French Minister for European Affairs made the point: 'It's clear that the new Europe will no longer be as homogeneous as the old one, that enlargement modifies the nature of European Union and that, in this context, elements of flexibility become essential'.

That 'flexibility' is the provisions in the 1997 Amsterdam Treaty which specifically allow for so-called 'enhanced co-operation' whereby if a majority of states in the Union wished to deepen their immersion with each other and carry forward still further the project of ever-closer union, they can do so – provided only that at least eight are involved and that they have the consent of those who are left outside.

In other words, the states that do not wish for 'enhanced co-operation' have been given a treaty veto. Not surprisingly, M Moscovici in his interview of 3 April indicated both that France wished to make use of 'the enhanced co-operation' procedures but that they 'were keen to remove the clause, on the need for the Council's authorisation which gives every member state a virtual veto on initiatives its partners might wish to take'.

Subsequent statements made by Prime Minister Jospin and President Chirac make it clear that the abolition of this veto will be among the changes pursued in the IGC that is to report to the Nice Summit.

Here indeed is a situation that a determined and competent British government, with some understanding of the wishes and interests of its own people, their institutions and their history, should grasp and through it establish a long-lasting, mutually agreeable and far more honest relationship with its continental neighbours.

The basic bargain is this: the UK will only agree to abolish the veto it possesses on moves towards 'enhanced co-operation' – or further integration – if at the same time the European Union Treaties are amended to allow for a tier of members, including both existing members and applicants, that can confine its obligations to those of a trade and economic treaty and, for political co-operation purposes, to a council of Europe.

If that genuinely 'fundamental renegotiation' were to fail, then of course the UK would be free to consider whether a different non-membership relationship would be preferred. The European Economic Zone Treaty, that includes Norway and Switzerland in an apparently perfectly satisfactory economic relationship with the European Union, may well be a model to be pursued.

But the point is this: we are free to choose. We do not have to belong to any trade grouping – other than the World Trade Organisation that establishes trading rules across the globe. When the British establishment lost its nerve in the early 1960s and desperately sought UK membership of the then Common Market, there was at least the case that the common external tariff that the Six were busily erecting imposed a duty of 12 per cent on foreign, including British, industrial goods. Successive negotiating rounds – the Kennedy round, the Uruguay round – have brought down that common external tariff to 3 to 4 per cent. And no doubt, the forthcoming Millennium round will achieve still further global tariff reductions.

But, already, a tariff that was once a high fence has become no more than a low garden wall. And when non-membership would relieve the United Kingdom of the obligations to buy high-cost Community food and re-establish connections with low-cost agriculture producers in Australasia, South America, Canada and the USA, the overall effect will certainly not be to our trading disadvantage. In addition, if we were to become non-members, we would cease to go on adding to that £40 billion plus net contribution to the funds of the European Union which we have paid so far since 1973 and which continues to cost us, net, at least £2 billion a year.

And that brings me to my *sixth* and penultimate conclusion. In resisting its integration within the emerging European Union state and maintaining its separate political identity, the UK is marching with, not against, the great movements of our time. In the same fifty years that have passed since Robert Schuman launched his European Coal and Steel Community idea, the world has been reshaped and convulsed by the triumph everywhere of the emergent nation state – and indeed the mini-state as well. The United Nations that was launched in 1946 with 52 members, has now 188.

Here is one of the great dynamic forces that has shaped and is continuing to shape our contemporary world: the wish, the passion, of people for self-government: to be ruled by those with whom they feel strong bonds of identity, culture, language – and equally, *not* to be ruled, however enlightened that rule may be, by those with whom they do not feel a close identity.

The great tide of sentiment that is backing the almost universal demand for self-government is itself being massively reinforced by a tide within that tide – the demand for democracy, for the rights of the peoples in self-governing states to be directly involved in the appointment and dismissal of their rulers.

This commitment to democracy is now the declared main external political objective – apart from resistance to armed aggression – not just of the United States, the United Kingdom, the old British Dominions and a handful of Scandinavian states, but of the whole Commonwealth, of the whole continent of South and Central America, of the countries of the European Union – and of many more.

In some countries, the process has yet to begin. In many more it is still imperfect and insecure. But there can be no doubt that the democratic process has been both extended and accelerated by the end of the Cold War. Oppressive and dictatorial regimes can no longer expect to be supported or indeed tolerated because they were reliable allies of either side in that struggle.

So, the twin doctrines of the nation state, self-government and democracy – and with democracy increasing respect for minorities and the rule of law – are becoming in this twenty first century the general rule and experience of the majority of mankind.

So far so good. But the second great requirement of our time is the further development of a rule of law, not just within states, but between states and their dealings with each other; and the further need of all, in a global economy, for effective means for maintaining and promoting prosperity; defending the environment from its many threats and catering for our still soaring human population.

And that brings me to my *seventh and last conclusion*. This new world of nation states requires global arrangements and institutions: their needs cannot, and will not, be met by regional organisations with their inevitably limited interests and perspectives, even by so powerful a body as the European Union.

The basic framework for a better and saner world and for the necessary international co-operation was laid down, not in the Rome Treaty, but in the Charter of the United Nations in 1945. And the main institutions, the specialised agencies for developing such co-operation in different sectors of human affairs were also established, along with the main political institutions, the General Assembly and the Security Council and the International Court of Justice that were empowered to establish and develop, and where necessary to enforce, the rule of international law.

That framework has endured and while its functioning was greatly limited by the near global rivalry of the old Soviet Union and the Western democracies, even then some considerable successes were achieved. In the post cold-war world, no longer divided and frustrated by the superpower rivalry of the Soviet Union and the USA, the role of the United Nations, and its effectiveness, can be and should be powerfully increased. Britain and its fellow Commonwealth members, fifty four no less, have an obviously important part to play in the General Assembly and in other international forums. And the United Kingdom itself has the particular strength and influence that goes with permanent membership of the Security Council and with the right of veto and of initiative that the permanent five possess.

This UN system clearly needs further development and strengthening – and the United Kingdom should certainly now bend its efforts, in co-operation with its partners and allies in the European Union, the Commonwealth and the English-speaking world, to that end.

And the first requirement is the vital need to safeguard peace and security against the threat and the reality of armed attack. We need both the reaffirmation of the doctrine of collective security, of the commitment to resist aggression, and the mobilisation of forces internationally to give these central undertakings the credibility they need. The world community of approaching 200 sovereign states that has developed over recent decades and which will certainly continue in the future, includes many militarily weak, vulnerable but resource-rich states. Some (e.g. Singapore and the Gulf States.) are well within reach of much more powerful neighbours. Their independence in the last resort needs the guarantee of the world community, a world community committed to enforce the basic principles of the UN charter.

Today, in spite of some post-Cold War successes, the forces available for UN peace enforcement missions have proved to be slow to mobilise, inadequate in fire power and, in some recent missions in parts of Africa, a failure.

The US, the power best equipped to organise, lead and finance UN-sanctioned armed force is, unhappily, reluctant, even hostile, to perform that leadership role. It does not want to be the world policeman – particularly when other nations contribute so marginally to collective enforcement measures. It is necessary therefore for those who believe in international order and, where necessary, its enforcement by military means, to make manifest their commitment to collective action.

The earmarking of 'rapid reaction' forces, dedicated to assist in Security Council-approved military expeditions – as negotiated by the UK with the UN in the 1999 memorandum of understanding – is just the sort of undertaking that is required. But there are limits to what Britain itself can, or should, do. Our diplomacy should be focused on persuading other nations to make arrangements similar to those that we have ourselves agreed. Success here would have a significant effect on US public opinion – for the US, providing it is sufficiently supported by its allies, has shown both in the NATO and European Areas – as well as the Gulf – a notable, if reluctant willingness to undertake military tasks: in the case of Kosovo, at the very margin of its own, narrowly conceived, national interest.

The other main development needed in this world of the twenty first century is the development of a new Economic and Financial Council, with a worldwide brief to identify and help combat the main threats to economic progress. Global institutions have now long existed with expertise, authority and resources to tackle aspects of the world economy: the World Bank, the International Monetary Fund, the Food and Agriculture Organisation, the International Labour Organisation, the World Trade Organisation and the World Environment Forum are among those that spring to mind. But, as has already been noted, what is clearly missing is an over-arching Council, with an inclusive economic/social/environmental remit. The Group of Seven – or Eight – has done some of the necessary work. But it needs developing to the point where it would become the focal point of reference, of guidance and co-ordinated action for dealing with problems that are simply too large for lesser, even large regional bodies, to tackle. A world economy based overwhelmingly on free markets in capital and trade and with giant multinational corpora-

235

tions does need at the minimum, organised counter-capitalist, inter-governmental pressures – better still the discipline of some effective regulatory power with a global reach.

Finally, both the Security Council of the United Nations and the Group of Seven – or Eight – need additional members to bring in those new power centres that have emerged since their own formation.

The only alternative and challenge to the development of such an *international* order, is the creation of a small number of powerful *regional* blocks, to defend and promote the collective interests of their members. That of course is the old, largely out-of-date vision of the European federalists, of those who shared Prime Minister Heath's belief that the future belonged to a 'world of giants' in which nation states would become redundant and international organisations and treaties would be largely replaced by a new balance of power between a handful of superstates.

Such a development is now highly unlikely – as well as being highly undesirable. It is highly unlikely because, in the world picture of the Euro federalists and Ted Heath, the future belonged to great power blocks including the then Soviet Union, the United States, Japan and later, China and India and – they hoped – a United Europe to sit by their side. The dissolution of the Soviet Union in 1991 and the clearly stronger tendency to dismember existing states rather than to merge states into still larger aggregates, is self-evident. That is simply not the way the world is going. As for the desirability of regional superblocks, if such a choice existed, there is a genuine danger that rivalry between them, competition for markets and resources, inadequate contact and understanding with areas outside their own, could lead to unnecessary divisions and estrangements between power blocks.

There is indeed a particular value to be attached to genuinely inter-national, rather than continental or regional associations and organisations, of which the United Nations itself and the

Commonwealth are the world's leading examples – if for no other reason than that they do bring together different cultures, different interests, different continents and different problems of security.

But there is a vitally important additional factor that argues against regionalism of the kind exemplified by the European Union. For its member states, it provides not just the defined constraints, rights and obligations that all treaties impose upon their signatories, but, in addition, it demonstrates acceptance of the authority of its specially created supranational institutions. These appointed, not elected, bodies are vested with the power not just to enforce treaty provisions but the right to develop and enlarge them as well. The powers of the nation states, the right of accountability and redress that democracy affords their people, is thus transferred to non-elected institutions. Thus has been established a new independent legal order and treaty-making power in the European Union, superior to the laws passed and decisions made in member states by their elected members of Parliament and their Ministers responsible to them.

Inevitably, the price paid for the benefits that supranational treaty arrangements confer, is the progressive loss of self-government: a growing democratic deficit is thus built into arrangements of this kind.

It is a heavy price to pay. Fortunately it does not have to be paid in order to achieve necessary inter-state agreements. The alternative is of course the normal bilateral, multi-lateral or international treaty which also involves defined constraints, obligations, rights and benefits. And no one can doubt the need for an increasing density and coverage of agreements between nation states in the more integrated world in which we live.

But such international treaties do *not* involve the transfer of law-making power and treaty-making power to external authorities. The rights of the democratic state and the parliaments and people within them are preserved.

Through their supranational treaties and institutions, the countries of the European Union have been driven into a non-democratic cul-de-sac.

Its only way out – but only for those to whom the existing relationships of peoples and governments is so close that there is no longer any serious sense of 'us' and 'them', but of near total identity – is to elect parliamentary institutions whose majority decisions can be accepted by minority peoples and states without any sense of being imposed upon.

In the years ahead, the Founding Six and some other European Union states may well, with the help of 'enhanced co-operation', sufficiently strengthen that new European identity that makes, 'ever-closer union' and a European state achievable.

It will not be easy, even for them. For the great bulk of mankind living in nation states both in the other continents of the world and indeed in Europe itself – many of whom are now achieving for the first time the goals of democracy and the rule of law together with self-government – it is an unattractive, even a repellent prospect.

For the United Kingdom and its people it is not merely unwanted: it is deeply repugnant and offensive. We don't want it. We don't need it. The goals that really matter – independence, democracy, security, relative prosperity and effective international co-operation – are well within our grasp. They are not even under threat.

To surrender such assets for an uncertain place inside the European state that is now so clearly emerging, would be an act not far short of madness and betrayal.

Further Reading

Over the years there has been a vast output of books on the UK and Europe. Those that I have listed below are chosen for two main reasons. First, because their authors (or those interviewed) have had direct, high level dealings with the European Community/European Union as politicians or diplomats. And second because they have written, from diverse points of view, worthwhile studies of the subject – and have done so recently – thus encompassing most of the relevant developments.

Paul Henri Spaak (1971)	*Memoirs: The Continuing Battle*
Uwe Kitzinger (1972)	*Diplomacy and Persuasion*
H.M. Gladwyn Jebb (1972)	*Memoirs*
Jean Monnet (1976)	*Memoirs*
Douglas Jay (1980)	*Change and Fortune*
Michael Charlton (1983)	*The Price of Victory*
Alistair Horne(1985)	*Macmillan*
Sir Nicholas Henderson	*Channels and Tunnels*
Margaret Thatcher (1993)	*Downing Street Years*
Charles Williams (1993)	*The Last Great Frenchman*
Eric Roll (1995	*Where Did We Go Wrong?*
Lionel Bell (1995)	*The Throw That Failed*
Sir Roy Denman (1996)	*Missed Chances*
Alistair McAlpine (1997)	*Once A Jolly Bagman*
Larkin and Oliver (1998)	*A Discreet Word: Britain's Secret Propaganda During the Cold War*
Hugo Young (1998)	*This Blessed Plot*
Peter Unwin (1998)	*Hearts, Minds and Interests*
Edward Heath (1998)	*The Course of My Life*
Stephen George (1998)	*An Awkward Partner* (3rd ed.)
Raymond Seitz (1998)	*Over Here*
John Major (1999)	*John Major: The Autobiography*
Norman Davies (1999)	*The Isles*
Larry Siedentop (2000)	*Democracy in Europe*

Index